Wole Soyinka

MADMEN
AND
SPECIALISTS

METHUEN DRAMA

A METHUEN MODERN PLAY

First published by Methuen and Co Ltd in 1971.
Reprinted in 1988 by Methuen London Ltd.

Reprinted in 1990 by Methuen Drama
an imprint of Reed International Books Ltd
Michelin House, 81 Fulham Road, London SW3 6RB
and Auckland, Melbourne, Singapore and Toronto

Reprinted 1991
Reissued with a new cover design 1993
Reprinted 1994, 1995, 1997

Copyright © 1971 by Wole Soyinka

ISBN 0–416–18760–9

The photograph on the front cover shows a scene from the original production by the University Theatre Company, Ibadan, and is reproduced by courtesy of J. G. Adetona.

Printed and bound in Great Britain by
Cox & Wyman Ltd, Reading, Berkshire

MADMEN AND SPECIALISTS

Dr Bero is a medical specialist who goes to the front as a doctor and there changes profession to become an intelligence specialist. The 'madmen' are Dr Bero's father and his followers in the mocking cult of 'As'. This is an ironic expression of horror not only at his own son's change of roles but at the universal triumph of expediency and power lust, which makes dehumanisation possible. Set in the context of war and its aftermath, the play is a powerful dramatic statement, perhaps more universal in its language and its application than Soyinka's previous works.

An early version of the play was written and staged in August 1970 during the Playwright's Workshop conference at the Eugene O'Neill Theater Center, Waterford, USA. This published version had its première at Ibadan, Nigeria, in March 1971.

Wole Soyinka was born in Nigeria in 1934. Educated there and at Leeds University, he worked in the British theatre before returning to West Africa in 1960, where he has since been based. In 1986 he became the first African writer to win the Nobel Prize for Literature. His plays include *The Jero Plays* (1960, 1966), *The Road* (1965), *The Lion and the Jewel* (1966), *Madmen and Specialists* (1971), *A Play of Giants* (1984), *A Scourge of Hyacinths* (1991) and *From Zia, With Love* (1992). His novels include *The Interpreters* (1973) and *Season of Anomy* (1980) and his collections of poetry include *Idanre* (1967), *A Shuttle in the Crypt* (1972), a volume of poems written during a period of over two years in prison without trial and *Mandela's Earth* (1990). His autobiographical volumes include *Aké, The Years of Childhood* (1981), *Ìsarà* (1989) and *Ibadan* (1994). His collections of essays, *Art, Dialogue and Outrage* was published in 1988.

MADMEN AND SPECIALISTS

The first version of *Madmen and Specialists* was performed at the 1970 Playwrights' Workshop Conference at the Eugene O'Neill Theater Center, Waterford, Connecticutt, U.S.A. The first complete version, printed here, had its première at the University of Ibadan, Nigeria, in March 1971, with the University Theatre Arts Company. The cast was as follows:

AAFAA		Femi Johnson
BLINDMAN	*Mendicants*	Femi Osofisan
GOYI		Wale Ogunyemi
CRIPPLE		Tunji Oyelana
SI BERO *Sister to Dr Bero*		Deola Adedoyin
IYA AGBA	*Two old Women*	Nguba Agolia
IYA MATE		Bopo George
DR BERO *Specialist*		Nat Okoro
PRIEST		Gbenga Sonuga
THE OLD MAN *Bero's Father*		Dapo Adelugba

Designed and directed by the author.

The action takes place in and around the home surgery of Dr Bero, lately returned from the wars.

Part One

Open space before BERO's *home and surgery. The surgery is down in a cellar. The level ground in the fore and immediate front space serve as drying space for assorted barks and herbs. The higher structure to one side is a form of semi-open hut. Inside it sit* IYA AGBA *and* IYA MATE. IYA AGBA *is smoking a thin pipe.* IYA MATE *stokes a small fire.*

By the roadside is a group of mendicants – CRIPPLE, GOYI, BLINDMAN *and* AAFAA. AAFAA's *St Vitus spasms are designed to rid the wayfarer of his last pennies in a desperate bid to be rid of the sight.* GOYI *is held stiffly in a stooping posture by a contraption which is just visible above his collar. The* CRIPPLE *drags on his knees. They pass the time by throwing dice from the gourd rattle.*

The CRIPPLE *has just thrown the dice.*

AAFAA. Six and four. Good for you.

CRIPPLE. Your turn, Blindman. (*Gives the dice and gourd to* BLINDMAN.)

    BLINDMAN *throws.*

Five and five. Someone is going to give us fivers.

GOYI. Fat chance of that. (*He throws.*)

AAFAA. Three and two, born loser. What did you stake?

GOYI. The stump of the left arm.

CRIPPLE. Your last?

GOYI. No, I've got one left.

BLINDMAN. Your last. You lost the right stump to me yesterday.

GOYI. Do you want it now or later?

BLINDMAN. Keep it for now.

CRIPPLE. When do I get my eye, Aafaa?

AAFAA. Was it the right or the left?

GOYI. Does it matter?

AAFAA. Sure it does. If it's the right one he can take it out now. The left is my evil eye and I need it a while longer.

CRIPPLE. It was the right.

AAFAA. I've just remembered the right is my evil eye.

CRIPPLE. I'll make you an offer. Let me throw against both of you for Goyi's stumps. I'll stake the eye Aafaa lost to me.

GOYI. Why leave me out? I still want to try my luck.

BLINDMAN. You have nothing left to stake.

CRIPPLE. You're just a rubber ball, Goyi. You need a hand to throw with, anyway.

GOYI. I can use my mouth.

AAFAA. To throw dice? You'll eat sand my friend.

BLINDMAN. Sooner or later we all eat sand.

CRIPPLE. Hey, you're beginning to sound like the Old Man.

AAFAA (*voice change*). Did you eat sand, my friend? We'll make you the Ostrich in our touring circus.

BLINDMAN. The limbless acrobat will now perform his wonderful act – how to bite the dust from three classic positions.

GOYI. Upright, take off, and prone.

CRIPPLE. We'll never go on that tour.

AAFAA. Roll up – roll up. Presenting the Creatures of As in the timeless parade.

BLINDMAN. Think we'll ever make that tour?

AAFAA. We will. But until the millions start rolling in, we better not neglect the pennies. (*He nudges them, pointing to* SI BERO.)

SI BERO *approaches, carrying a small bag from which protrude some twigs with leaves and berries. The* MENDICANTS *begin their performance as soon as they sense her approach.* BLINDMAN *is alms collector,* GOYI *repeats a single acrobatic trick,* AAFAA *is the 'dancer'.* BLINDMAN *shakes the rattles while the* CRIPPLE *drums with his crutches and is lead singer.* BLINDMAN *collects alms in the rattles.*

SI BERO (*as* AAFAA *moves to intercept her*). Don't try that nonsense with me. I live in this neighbourhood, remember?

AAFAA (*his spasms ceasing abruptly. The others also stop playing*). Don't they say charity begins at home?

SI BERO. Your preaching is so good it's a wonder you can't find yourself a congregation.

AAFAA (*stiffening*). What congregation, woman? Who said I was ever a preacher?

SI BERO. You were never anything. Go and find some decent work to do.

AAFAA. With this affliction of mine?

SI BERO. It comes and goes, not so? You can work in between.

AAFAA. And this one? And that? And that? (*Pointing lastly to* GOYI.) If it weren't for the iron rod holding up his spine he would collapse like a toad you step on. Just what sort of work do you want him to do?

GOYI. A penny or two, Si Bero. We haven't eaten today.

BLINDMAN. And that is God's truth. Aafaa, why do you pick a quarrel with her? Just ask her for a few pennies, you know she treats us well.

CRIPPLE. The lane is deserted. Nobody comes and goes any more.

GOYI. Something is driving them away from here. If there isn't something going on, then this isn't an iron I have in my back.

AAFAA. It is your neighbourhood, you say, Si Bero. What are you doing to drive people away?

SI BERO. Perhaps your mother's ghost is haunting the place. Why don't you ask her the next time she visits you?

AAFAA. Why do you always pick on me, old woman? What has my mother done to you?

SI BERO. She gave birth to you for a start. (*She throws a penny to the* CRIPPLE *who tosses it into the gourd.*) If you want more than that, you know where to come. I still need people to sort out my herbs.

AAFAA. Herbs! Herbs! Herbs! Always – come and sort out herbs to earn yourself a decent coin.

SI BERO. And eat. You can have work and eat. The two go together.

She goes out.

CRIPPLE (*throwing the coin in the gourd, calls after her*). God bless you, Si Bero.

BLINDMAN. He shall, he will, he must.

GOYI. He'd better or I'll know the reason why.

CRIPPLE. Your turn, Aafaa.

AAFAA. What for?

CRIPPLE. A penny is something.

AAFAA. Not for me.

GOYI. Give her a pennyworth, then.

AAFAA. Can't be bothered.

BLINDMAN. Go on. Don't be mean.

CRIPPLE. You're the priest, after all.

AAFAA (*suddenly grinning*). A penny's worth, you say?

CRIPPLE. That's only fair.

AAFAA (*shouting after the now distant woman*). God bless your brother!

They all break out guffawing.

GOYI. More grease to his elbow.

AAFAA. Not forgetting his armpits.

BLINDMAN. More power to his swagger-stick!

CRIPPLE. May light ever shine . . .

AAFAA. From his braids and buttons.

GOYI. May he come home safely . . .

AAFAA. To your loving arms.

CRIPPLE. Not to mention his Daddy's.

GOYI. God help her, that is some brother she has. You may say he is . . . dutiful.

CRIPPLE. Him a dutiful son? You're crazy.

BLINDMAN. I know what he means. (*He points an imaginary gun.*) Bang! All in the line of duty!

 GOYI *clutches his chest, slumps over.*

AAFAA. Did we try him?

CRIPPLE. Resurrect, you fool. Nobody tried you yet.

AAFAA (*in a ringing voice*). You are *accused.*

BLINDMAN. Satisfied?

CRIPPLE. Fair enough.

BLINDMAN. Bang!

 GOYI *slumps.*

AAFAA (*rinsing his hands*). Nothing to do with me.

BLINDMAN. Fair trial, no?

AAFAA. Decidedly yes.

BLINDMAN. What does he say himself?

GOYI. Very fair, gentlemen. I have no complaints.

BLINDMAN. In that case we permit you to be buried.

GOYI. You are generous, gentlemen. I have a personal aversion to vultures.

BLINDMAN. Oh, come come. Nice birds they are. They clean up after the mess.

CRIPPLE. Not like some bastards we know. (*He spits.*)

AAFAA (*posing*). In a way you may call us vultures. We clean up the mess made by others. The populace should be grateful for our presence. (*He turns slowly round.*) If there is anyone here who does not approve us, just say so and we quit. (*His hand makes the motion of half-drawing out a gun.*) I mean, we are not here because we like it. We stay at immense sacrifice to ourselves, our leisure, our desires, vocation, specialization, etcetera, etcetera. The moment you say, Go, we . . . (*He gives another inspection all round, smiles broadly and turns to the others.*) They insist we stay.

CRIPPLE. I thought they would. Troublesome little insects but . . . they have a sense of gratitude. I mean, after all we did for them.

GOYI. And still do.

BLINDMAN. And will continue to do.

CHORUS. Hear hear hear hear. Very well said, sir.

GOYI. Oh, come on. Shall we follow the woman or yap here all day? Let's get spying.

AAFAA. She's a devil, that's my complaint. She was born with a stone in her stomach.

GOYI. What's wrong? It's the job we are here to do, isn't it?

AAFAA. I still don't like messing about with her herbs.

BLINDMAN. Herbs are herbs, not so? Let's get going.

AAFAA. That woman's herbs are not just herbs. She hoards them and treats them like children. The whole house is full of twigs. If it's a straightforward business, why doesn't she use them? Or sell them or something?

GOYI. But everyone knows she's mad. They get that way after a while living alone. I've known one woman in my village who collects potsherds. Any piece of broken pot would do. Just let an old woman live by herself for a short while and she gets up to all sorts of things. Boxes, cupboards, trunks, every nook and corner. You couldn't walk on the floor without crunching pottery under your foot. Then she would scream curses at you.

CRIPPLE. What are we to do?

GOYI. There must be some way to stay nearer the house most of the day. We can't spend the whole day sorting herbs.

AAFAA. She's a witch. When she spirits out a foetus from the belly of a pregnant woman she pickles it in the herbs and it goes in a bottle for her brother's experiments.

BLINDMAN. For a so-called chaplain you talk plenty of nonsense.

AAFAA. Listen to the blind fool. What do you know about it?

CRIPPLE. Are we going to argue or follow her home?

GOYI. I don't like the whole business. She has been good to us.

AAFAA. With the pennies she throws as if she's feeding a dog? I spit on that kind of goodness!

CRIPPLE. I still don't like it. Why is he doing it? His own family too, what's he up to?

GOYI. He's a specialist.

AAFAA. Amen.

GOYI. What?

AAFAA. Amen. He is a specialist. That takes care of everything, not so?

GOYI. There is bound to be something in it for us.

BLINDMAN. Something like burnt fingers?

GOYI. What do you mean?

BLINDMAN (*shrugs*). When things go wrong it's the lowest who get it first.

AAFAA. There is money at the bottom of it.

CRIPPLE (*places* BLINDMAN's *hand on his shoulder and starts off in the direction of the house*). And we are at the bottom. So, let's go and make sure the woman doesn't stumble on any official secrets.

AAFAA (*checks*). Rem Acu Tetigisti.

CRIPPLE. What? I don't get you.

AAFAA. R.A.T.! R.A.T.! I smell a rat.

GOYI. Is he having an attack?

CRIPPLE. What's up, Aafaa?

AAFAA. You said it yourself – Official Secrets. Official rat is what I smell. Yessir! We'll get paid something decent. Secret Service funds and all that. Let's celebrate.

GOYI. Nonsense. It's just a simple family vendetta.

AAFAA. Christ! Every one of you freaks will have ideas! And where did you pick up that word, anyway?

GOYI. Where you pick up yours, leave me alone.

AAFAA (*haughtily*). One thing I disapproved of in the Old Man was he didn't discriminate. Talk of casting pearls before swine. Vendetta my foot. I tell you the Cripple has Rem Acu Tetigistied it. Official Secrets that's what's at the bottom of it. Bottomless account. We'll get overtime and risk allowance.

GOYI. It's not going to be risky, is it?

AAFAA. I know you have none, but I'll be risking my conscience. That needs compensation.

CRIPPLE. What do you think, Blindman?

BLINDMAN. Hm. Aafaa may be right. For once.

AAFAA. Never mind the cleverness. You agree.

BLINDMAN. R.A.T. You have touched the matter with a needle.

GOYI. Where? I'm still lost.

AAFAA. Where? I'll soon show you, dumbclod. (*He lunges for* GOYI's *crotch.*)

GOYI (*protecting himself*). No!

AAFAA. Why not? You got any more use for it?

BLINDMAN. Maybe he wants to continue the line.

AAFAA. What! This crooked line? It would be a disservice to humanity.

CRIPPLE. Hey. Think he'll do that to his own father?

BLINDMAN. When the Specialist wants results badly enough...

CRIPPLE. Yes, but what results?

AAFAA. Does it matter? (*Voice change. He points a 'needle' held low, at* GOYI.) Say anything, say anything that comes into your head but SPEAK, MAN! (*Twisting the needle upwards.*)

GOYI, *hand over crotch, yells.*

BLINDMAN (*solemnly*). Rem Acu Tetigisti.

AAFAA. Believe me, this hurts you more than it hurts me. Or – vice versa. Truth hurts. I am a lover of truth. Do you find you also love truth? Then let's have the truth. THE TRUTH! (*He gives another push.* GOYI *screams.*)

CRIPPLE.
BLINDMAN. } Rem Acu Tetigisti.

AAFAA. Think not that I hurt you but that Truth hurts. We are all seekers after truth. I am a Specialist in truth. Now shall we push it up all the way, all the way? Or shall we have all the truth all the truth. (*Another push.* GOYI *screams, then his head slumps.*) Hm, the poor man has fainted.

CRIPPLE.
BLINDMAN.
} Rem Acu Tetigisti.

> AAFAA *makes a motion of slapping his face several times.*
> GOYI *revives.*

GOYI. Where am I?

CRIPPLE. Within the moment of truth, dear friend.

AAFAA (*chanting*). Rem Acu ...

OTHERS. Tetigisti, tetigisti.

ALTOGETHER. Rem Acu Tetigisti.

AAFAA. You have touched it with a ...

OTHERS. Fine needle, fine fine needle.

ALL. You have touched it with a fine fine.

AAFAA. Rem Acu ...

> *They repeat the song,* AAFAA *singing Rem Acu Tetigisti in
> counterpoint to the others* 'You have touched it with a
> needle'.

Hey. (*He taps* GOYI *on the shoulder.*) Are you recovered?
Good. Here we go again.

CRIPPLE. Perhaps he needs a drink of water.

AAFAA. Really? Well, give him one, then. We are no monsters
here. No one will charge me with heartlessness. Give him a
drink of water. A large one.

> BLINDMAN *hands* GOYI *a 'bowl' of water.* GOYI *drains it
> while they all watch avidly.*

Satisfied? Happy? More? No. (*He takes the bowl and hands it
to* BLINDMAN.) Anything else? Perhaps you would like to
use the conveniences? The toilet? (GOYI *nods.*) Over there.
Be my guest.

> GOYI *turns, his hand goes to his fly, he stops, turns round
> slowly. A big grin appears on the faces of the other three.*

What's the matter? No wan' pee-pee? Pee-pee pee-pee?
No more pee-pee? I know what it is. (*Chanting.*) Rem Acu ...

OTHERS. Tetigisti, tetigisti . . .

As they go through the chant again SI BERO *reappears with a small bunch of herbs. They quickly stop singing.*

CRIPPLE. Are we to come now, Si Bero? We need the work.
SI BERO. Wait here. I'll tell you when I'm ready.

They watch her pass. She goes into the OLD WOMEN's *hut and* AAFAA *sneaks near a moment later, to try and eavesdrop. The others pass the time throwing dice.*
In the OLD WOMEN's *hut.*

IYA MATE. A-ah, you have a good eye, daughter.
IYA AGBA. Where did you find it?
SI BERO. Not far from where I went yesterday. Someone had emptied a pile of rubbish near by, that's why I missed it.

The two OLD WOMEN *move nearer the light, examining the berries.*

IYA MATE. The berries are all right too. Birds attack them quite early. You are lucky.
IYA AGBA. I wasn't expecting her to find any berries.
SI BERO (*dipping in the bag*). I brought you some tobacco. And snuff for you, Iya Mate.
IYA MATE. You are a good woman. Some menfolk leave the home and never know whether they will come back to a dung-heap or worse.
IYA AGBA. Weeds growing through the window and bats hanging from the rafters. That is when they find out that some women carry a curse in their breasts.
IYA MATE. Your menfolk are lucky. There will be leaves in their living-room – but not the kind that places the handprint of death on a man's heart. Now, you leave these here.
IYA AGBA (*suddenly*). Let me see that. Let me see it!
IYA MATE. What's the matter?
IYA AGBA. Bring it here. It's not the right one at all.

IYA MATE. Here. Look for yourself. No one can tell me my
eyes are failing.

IYA AGBA. Just now I remember what you said – birds haven't
attacked it. Usually it's the poison kind they don't go near.
(*She breaks the stalk.*) I thought so. This is the twin. Poison.

SI BERO. Poison! But . . .

IYA MATE. It can't be poison.

IYA AGBA. They don't grow much. Haven't seen one in – oh,
since I was a child. Farmers destroy them as soon as they
see them. But it's the poison twin all right. Except for that
red streak along the stalk you wouldn't tell them apart.

IYA MATE. I didn't even know there was the poison kind.

IYA AGBA. You don't see them much. Once in a lifetime.
Farmers don't let them live, you know. Burn out the soil
where they find it growing, just to kill the seeds. Foolish-
ness. Poison has its uses too. You can cure with poison if
you use it right. Or kill.

SI BERO. I'll throw it in the fire.

IYA MATE. Do nothing of the sort. You don't learn good
things unless you learn evil.

SI BERO. But it's poison.

IYA MATE. It grows.

IYA AGBA. Rain falls on it.

IYA MATE. It sucks the dew.

IYA AGBA. It lives.

IYA MATE. It dies.

IYA AGBA. Same as any other. An-hn, same as any other.

SI BERO. That means I still have to find the right one.

IYA AGBA. It will be in the same place. They grow together
most of the time.

SI BERO. I'll go tomorrow.

IYA MATE. Take some rest. Or . . . is he on his way home?

SI BERO. There is no news at all. I am beginning to . . .

IYA AGBA. Beginning to worry like every foolish woman. He'll
come back. He and his father. There is too much binds

them down here. They will take root with their spirit, not with their bodies on some unblessed soil. Let me see your hands. (*She scrutinizes the hands carefully, bursts suddenly into a peal of laughter.*) These hands are not yet ready to wind shrouds. We shall drink palm wine soon, very soon when someone returns. (*She takes* SI BERO *by both hands and begins to shuffle with her, singing.*)

Ofe gbe wa de'le o – Ofe . . .
Ofe gbe wa de'le o – Ofe
Oko epo epa i runa
Gbe wa dele o
Ofe gbe wa de'le

> The MENDICANTS *look at one another, begin to beat time with them, then join the singing in a raucous, cynical tone. The* WOMEN *stop, amazed and offended. The* OLD WOMEN *fold their arms, retire deeper into the hut while* SI BERO *dashes out, furious.*

SI BERO. Stop that noise! Did I ask you here for entertainment?

CRIPPLE. No offence, Si Bero, no offence. We only thought you had forgotten us.

SI BERO. And thought your horrible voices the best way of reminding me.

GOYI. It's not our fault our voices are no better.

AAFAA. We can't all have voices like choiring angels, you know.

SI BERO. That's enough from you. Come along if you still want to work, only keep your voices down and stop frightening the neighbourhood.

> *They follow her to the front of the house.*

CRIPPLE. So here we are, Si Bero. Bring out the herbs and let us catch the smell of something in your kitchen while we are about it.

AAFAA. How much are we getting today? Let's decide that first.

SI BERO. Depends how hard you work.

GOYI. Let's start work. It's a hot day and a man may as well stay close to shelter.

SI BERO. I have a whole sack my buyer brought in yesterday.

She takes hold of BLINDMAN's *hand.*

You can give me a hand, the sack is heavy. (AAFAA *immediately positions himself to accompany her.*) Not you, damn your forwardness. Did I talk to you?

AAFAA. He's not much use. He'll trip over and break his neck.

SI BERO. And that's his business not yours.

She leads BLINDMAN *into the house.*

AAFAA. Did you see that?

GOYI. I am sure even the Blindman did.

CRIPPLE. She didn't want any of us three, that was certain, but I . . .

AAFAA. Picks the one who can't see a thing.

CRIPPLE. I saw.

AAFAA. I told you it's funny business.

CRIPPLE. I am trying to tell you I saw. I saw the herbs.

AAFAA. Where? Where?

CRIPPLE. From here. From down here I could see through a gap in the door when she opened it.

AAFAA. What then? What did you see?

CRIPPLE. Herbs. Roots. Nothing but dried plants. The shelves are right up to the ceiling and they were full of leaves. All browned and crinkled.

GOYI. What kind?

CRIPPLE. All kinds.

GOYI. What is she going to do with all that forest?

AAFAA. Perhaps now you will learn to listen to me.

CRIPPLE. She must be slightly crazy. Living all alone, I suppose.

AAFAA. S-sh. They're coming. See if you can sneak another look.

> SI BERO *and* BLINDMAN *enter, carrying a heavy sack between them.*

SI BERO (*entering backwards, she stumbles against the* CRIPPLE *who is trying to see through a crack*). Get out of the way, will you. Are you now the doorstop that I must step on you to get out of my own house?

CRIPPLE (*forced to retreat*). You are in a bad mood today, Si Bero.

SI BERO. Your mother is in a bad mood, not me. Now get working instead of dragging yourself in people's way. Get busy. You know how I like them sorted out.

AAFAA. Yes, we know.

GOYI. First the roots.

CRIPPLE. Then peel the barks.

AAFAA. Slice the stalks.

CRIPPLE. Squeeze out the pulps.

GOYI. Pick the seeds.

AAFAA. Break the pods. Crack the plaster.

CRIPPLE. Probe the wound or it will never heal.

BLINDMAN. Cut off one root to save the other.

AAFAA. Cauterize.

CRIPPLE. Quick-quick-quick-quick, amputate!

> BLINDMAN *lets out a loud groan.*

AAFAA. What do you mean, sir! How dare you lie there and whine?

GOYI. Cut his vocal chords.

AAFAA. 'Before we operate we cut the vocal chords.'

BLINDMAN. That's only for the dogs.

CRIPPLE. Your case is worse. You are an underdog.

GOYI. Rip out his vocal chords.

BLINDMAN *lets out another scream.*

AAFAA. We don't want you in this fraternity.

CRIPPLE. Fool! You should see the others and thank your stars.

BLINDMAN. I can't see them to thank.

AAFAA (*snatches his stick*). Shall I put them on his head? He can have them in all colours.

CRIPPLE. Leave him for now, we'll simply expel him.

BLINDMAN (*screaming again*). Oh God!

GOYI. Who's got the flaming sword?

AAFAA. Right here, Lord, right here.

GOYI. Show him the door.

AAFAA. Out of the garden, bum, don't ever show your face in here again.

BLINDMAN. I appeal.

CRIPPLE. Who to?

BLINDMAN. As.

AAFAA. In the name of As of the beginning, out!

BLINDMAN. No!

AAFAA. Out!

BLINDMAN. No!

AAFAA. One – Two – Three – Four —

BLINDMAN (*druggedly*). Five – Six – Seven – Eight – Nine —

AAFAA. Out!

BLINDMAN (*wearily*). Out! (*His head drops down.* AAFAA *raises the 'sword'.*)

SI BERO. Have you all gone mad?

AAFAA. No. I'm quite good at it, actually. One stroke and – clean through the tendons. Bang through the ball-and-socket, believe me. I never touch the marrow.

GOYI. Heh, stop. The woman.

SI BERO. I said have you gone mad? Are you here to work or fool around?

CRIPPLE. Oh, never mind us. Come on.

> *They settle down quickly. As the sack is emptied on the ground,* SI BERO, *already about to turn into the house, stops, goes over and picks out a bunch of roots which she turns about in her hand, inspecting it. The* MENDICANTS *cannot contain their curiosity, directly observing her action.* BLINDMAN *listens intensely into the silence. Finally she starts towards the* OLD WOMEN'S *hut.*

AAFAA. We can sort that bunch if you like. And give it a scraping. It seems dirty enough.

SI BERO (*turns slowly on him*). Not half as dirty as your anus. The day you scrape that you can tell me what needs scraping and what doesn't.

AAFAA (*raising his stick*). You go too far with that mouth of yours!

> SI BERO *looks him up and down contemptuously. She continues on her way.*

I have a mind to set fire to every single herb in that house.

BLINDMAN. Why don't you learn to leave her alone?

AAFAA. What did I do? What did I say? Just because of one stinking root. She has a mouth like a running gutter.

BLINDMAN. Leave the woman alone. She minds her own business, you mind yours.

AAFAA. And that's enough from you, Mr Blind Advocate. I don't have to listen to you take her side all the time. One more word from you . . .

> *He feints a slap across* BLINDMAN'S *face.* BLINDMAN, *alert, springs suddenly backwards and grasps his staff.* AAFAA *looks at him a moment, then bursts out laughing.*

Do you see what I see? The man actually wants to fight me. Did you see? Did you see him? He has no eyes but he actually wants to fight. Hm? Is it really a fight you're looking for, Blind One?

He kicks aside his staff but BLINDMAN *immediately closes in on* AAFAA, *reaches for his arms and imprisons them. They strain against each other.*

CRIPPLE. Bloody fools!

GOYI. Look! The specialist.

He points to the spot where they were first seen. Standing there is BERO, *uniformed, carrying a hold-all. He watches. The* CRIPPLE *tugs at the clothes of the struggling men.*

CRIPPLE. Better stop that, he's here.

GOYI. He's waiting for us. Come on.

The two men break apart. AAFAA *is panting heavily. The* CRIPPLE *dashes quickly and brings* BLINDMAN *his stick. Somewhat sheepishly they troop towards* BERO.

BERO (*gives them a long cold stare*). Was that what I sent you to do in that house?

AAFAA. He started it. And the woman.

CRIPPLE. Aafaa hit him first. Knocked off his stick. A blind man too.

He spits.

AAFAA. If people know they have a handicap then they shouldn't open their mouths to provoke their betters.

CRIPPLE. Hits a blind man. (*He spits again.*)

AAFAA. If you think just because you are a cripple you won't get it from me if you go beyond bounds, just try it and see.

CRIPPLE. A blind man. (*He spits again.*)

AAFAA (*raises the rattle threateningly*). Don't think because of him being here I can't . . .

The CRIPPLE *counters immediately by raising his crutch.*

BERO. Shut up! Shut up all of you. I didn't send you to the house to fight. I asked you to keep your eyes open and keep her from going down. (*He looks at them with contempt, then jerks his thumb in the direction of the cellar.*) What about him. Is he staying quiet?

AAFAA (*jerking his thumb at* BLINDMAN). Ask him. He is the only one who got to enter the house. Ask Blindman what he saw.

BERO. I have no time for fooling.

BLINDMAN. He was quiet. I don't think the woman knows anything.

BERO. What room did you enter?

BLINDMAN. The one with the herbs. I don't think there are any bare walls in there; it's all covered with herbs. From the floor to the ceiling, it's all full of herbs very carefully laid and touched and dusted every day of her life. I could tell that as soon as I entered.

CRIPPLE. I saw it. I caught a glimpse.

AAFAA. Last night when we got him into that underground place she was fast asleep. We didn't make a noise.

BLINDMAN. Excuse me, I wish to say something.

BERO. Yes?

BLINDMAN. I can only tell you what I felt – in that room where I stood with her. There is more love in there than you'll find in the arms of a hundred women. I don't know what unhappiness you intend for her but . . .

BERO. That's enough. You don't know a thing about anything, so shut up.

BLINDMAN *shrugs and retires to one side.*

GOYI. My feeling is, I can't help agreeing with him. In any case we are not much use to anyone.

BERO. I said that's enough. You're under orders.

AAFAA. I am not. And I haven't eaten today.

BERO. Very good.

AAFAA. Enh? Say that again. Which of what is very good?

BERO. The fact that you haven't eaten today. If you fall down on the job you know you will go back to being hungry.

AAFAA. Good. I am glad to hear where we stand. We've done one thing already and don't think it was easy getting him in

that hole without waking the neighbours or your sister. So
what about for now? Have we already fallen down on the
job that we see nothing of what you promised?

BERO (*studies him for a while, then turns to the others*). Have you
told him who I am exactly?

AAFAA. Oh yes, Dr Bero. I know who you are. The specialist.
We all do. So what about it? You say we are under orders
but I tell you I am not. I know these three are discharged.
As for me, I have never even taken orders from you before.

BERO. These are no longer discharged and you now take orders
from me. You either get that into your twisted mind or get
out now.

AAFAA. You can't tell me to get out. We teamed together
without your help and we are not doing badly as it is. You
can't come here and break us up. If we have anybody to
thank it's him down there. Not that I care. I always thought
he was crazy. But just don't you forget we are a team – one
for all and all for one.

BERO. You prefer that? Begging for pennies and getting spat
upon?

AAFAA. That's what you think. Ho ho, that's a good one, isn't
it? Isn't it? You don't know anything about us, do you?
Think we spent all that time with your old man without
learning a thing or two? You can't specialize in everything,
you know.

GOYI. Shut up, Aafaa.

CRIPPLE. You talk too much, shut your mouth.

BERO. He's saying nothing I don't know already.

AAFAA. You know nothing, Dr Bero. You can't bluff me.

BLINDMAN. You really are a fool, Aafaa.

CRIPPLE (*whining*). Pay no attention to him. We do nothing
really bad, just one or two things to eke out the droppings of
charity.

BERO. Save that for your customers. I'm not interested in
what you've done. But from now on you stop taking any

risks. I don't want to have to look for you in every filthy gaol.

CRIPPLE. If you'll make up for our losses, sir . . . we were on our way to greater things.

GOYI. I'll say that for us. We were just beginning.

BERO. To do what?

CRIPPLE. Well, you know . . . your Old Man did come up with some ripe ideas . . .

BERO. You'll be taken care of. That's a promise.

CRIPPLE. Then as I said before, that's all right by me.

GOYI. Me too.

AAFAA. No, it isn't. I don't mind the risks we are taking right now . . .

BERO. I said, no more risks.

AAFAA. That's for us to decide until you say how much. What does he know about risks anyway? Even if I was only a chaplain to the men out there I knew what risk was. I nearly had it once or twice. Quite different from working for Intelligence where all you had to do was sift through papers full of lies and know how to slap people around . . .

> BERO *cuts him across the face with his swagger stick.* AAFAA *staggers back, clutching the wound.* BERO *stands still, watching him. At the sound of pain* IYA AGBA *looks out of the hut and impassively observes the scene.*

BERO. That should remind you I do know how to slap people around. And you'd better remember some other things I know. You weren't just discharged because of your – sickness. Just remember that . . . and other things.

> *He stands gazing towards the house for a while.*

I am due home now. You know when to follow. Just remember to carry out my instructions to the letter.

> *He walks purposefully to the house. As he passes by the* OLD WOMEN's *hut* IYA AGBA *leans back to avoid being*

seen by him. A moment later SI BERO *emerges, sees* BERO *and shouts, running towards him.* IYA MATE *joins the other women to watch the reunion.*

SI BERO. Bero! Bero! (*She embraces him, then tears herself off and shouts.*)

BERO. Don't do that!

SI BERO (*rushing about, she doesn't hear*). He's home! He's . . .

BERO (*chases after and restrains her*). Be quiet!

SI BERO. What?

BERO. I don't want my return announced.

SI BERO. Why not? (*Suddenly suspicious.*) You're not going back again, are you?

BERO. It isn't that. I want some quiet, that's all.

SI BERO. Oh! how thoughtless I was. But they will be disappointed.

BERO. Who will?

SI BERO. Our neighbours. All your old patients.

BERO. Corpses.

SI BERO. What? I said your old patients.

BERO. I said corpses. Oh, forget it.

SI BERO. I can't. (*She scans his face anxiously.*) They haven't forgotten you.

BERO. They still exist, do they?

SI BERO (*again puzzled*). Who? I don't understand.

BERO. I'm tired. Let's talk of something else.

SI BERO. Oh yes, you must be. Come inside. No, wait. You mustn't come in yet. Be patient now, Bero. (*Hurrying into the house.*) Don't move from there. Stand still.

BERO *looks slowly round him, he gazes as if he is trying to pierce through walls into neighbouring homes. The expression on his face is contempt.*

SI BERO *reappears with a gourd of palm wine, pours it on the ground in front of the doorstep. Then she moves to unlace his boots.*

BERO. You still keep up these little habits.

SI BERO. I like to keep close to earth.

BERO (*stepping back to prevent her from taking off his boots*). Bare feet, wet earth. We've wetted your good earth with something more potent than that, you know.

SI BERO. Not you. Neither you nor Father. You had nothing to do with it. On the contrary.

BERO. What, on the contrary?

SI BERO. Were you together? Did you manage to work together?

BERO. We were together. For some time.

SI BERO. Is he going to stay with us?

BERO. We'll . . . discuss him later.

SI BERO (*suddenly fearful*). What is it, Bero? Is he . . . ?

BERO (*stares back at her, letting the pause hang*). Well, is he – what?

SI BERO (*laughing*). Stop trying to frighten me.

BERO. Who's trying to?

SI BERO. Where are you hiding him? I bet he's waiting round the corner.

BERO. He'll rejoin us in his own time.

SI BERO (*disappointed*). Oh. But he's safe.

BERO (*impatiently*). Of course he is.

SI BERO (*takes his hand*). Come with me. I must show you to the Old Women and tell them also Father is safe.

BERO. What Old Women?

SI BERO. Over there in the hut.

BERO. Who are they?

SI BERO. Herbalists. They helped me with your work.

BERO. But why bring them here? Why camp them on my door-step?

SI BERO. They were good to me. I couldn't have done a thing without them. Come and talk to them.

> BERO *does not move. Immediately, the* OLD WOMEN *start to speak.* BERO *and* SI BERO *remain still,* BERO *looking towards the* OLD WOMEN's *hut while* SI BERO *watches him.*

IYA AGBA. Well, has it been worth it, do you think?

IYA MATE. It's good to see her face bubbling like froth on good wine.

IYA AGBA. Not her, him!

IYA MATE. Oh, him. Well, you never can tell with seeds. The plant may be good . . . but we'll know, we'll know.

IYA AGBA. I hope it's a good seed. That was two lives we poured into her hands. Two long lives spent pecking at secrets grain by grain.

IYA MATE. More than two. What she took from us began with others we no longer call by name.

IYA AGBA. She sucked my head dry.

IYA MATE. She is a good woman.

IYA AGBA. Yes, but what about him?

IYA MATE. You sense something wrong in him?

IYA AGBA. It's my life that's gone into his. I haven't burrowed so deep to cast good earth on worthless seeds.

IYA MATE. Nor she. Tramping through all those bushes, finding the desolate spots only we remember.

IYA AGBA. She was stubborn, others would have given up early. (*She giggles.*) I did my best to put her off. Sent her on those fruitless errands, hoping she'd give up. Others would have done.

IYA MATE. Oh, you are wicked.

IYA AGBA. She proved herself, there's no denying it. She proved herself. If she'd wanted it easy or simply out of greed I would have guided her feet into quicksands and left her there.

IYA MATE. You would, I know you, you would.

IYA AGBA. So let him watch it. I haven't come this far to put my whole being in a sieve.

She turns abruptly and returns into the hut. IYA MATE *remains for a while.*

SI BERO. They told me what to look for, where to look for it. How to sort them and preserve them.

BERO (*nods*). You haven't wasted your time. I still need things from my former vocation.

SI BERO. Former vocation?

BERO. A means, not an end.

SI BERO. We heard terrible things. So much evil. Then I would console myself that I earned the balance by carrying on your work. One thing cancels out another. Bero, they're waiting. Go and greet them Bero. They held your life together while you were away.

BERO. What is that supposed to mean?

SI BERO. I never feared for you while they were here.

BERO. You really disappoint me. You are supposed to be intelligent. It was you I asked to do my work, not some stupid old hags. I suppose they filled your hand with all that evil stuff. You've been pretty free with that word.

SI BERO. Not you yourself Bero, but guilt contaminates. And often I was afraid . . . (*Suddenly determined.*) Bero, where is Father!?

BERO. Safe.

SI BERO (*stubbornly*). But you must know when he's coming.

BERO. Sometime.

SI BERO. When? Why didn't you return together?

BERO. He's a sick man. He is coming home to be cured.

SI BERO. Sick? Wounded?

BERO. Mind sickness. We must be kind to him.

SI BERO. How long, Bero? How long had he been sick?

BERO. Ever since he came out. Maybe the . . . suffering around him proved too much for him. His mind broke under the strain.

SI BERO (*quietly*). How bad? Don't hide anything, Bero. How bad is he?

BERO. He started well. But of course we didn't know which way his mind was working. Madmen have such diabolical cunning. It was fortunate I had already proved myself. He was dangerous. Dangerous!

SI BERO. What do you mean? Did he endanger you?

BERO. Did he! He was in a different sector, working among the convalescents. I wouldn't have known what was going on if I had still been with the Medical Corps.

SI BERO. If you had still been?

BERO. I told you. I switched.

SI BERO. But how? You have your training. How does one switch, just like that?

BERO. You are everything once you go out there. In an emergency . . . (*He shrugs.*) The head of the Intelligence Section died rather suddenly. Natural causes.

SI BERO. And that's the new vocation?

BERO. None other, sister, none other. The Big Braids agreed I was born into it. Not that that was any recommendation. They are all submental apes.

SI BERO (*studying him avidly, a slow apprehension beginning to show on her face*). But you have . . . you have given that up now. You are back to your real work. Your practice.

BERO (*turns calmly to meet her gaze*). Practice? Yes, I intend to maintain that side of my practice. A laboratory is important. Everything helps. Control, sister, control. Power comes from bending Nature to your will. The Specialist they called me, and a specialist is – well – a specialist. You analyse, you diagnose, you – (*He aims an imaginary gun.*) – prescribe.

SI BERO (*more to herself*). You should have told me. I have made pledges I cannot fulfil.

BERO. Pledges? What are you talking about?

SI BERO. I swore I was sure of you, only then would they help me.

BERO. Who? The Old Women?

SI BERO. They held nothing back from me.

The PRIEST *enters, hails them from a distance.*

PRIEST. A-ah, there you are. Bero, my boy, welcome home. I caught a glimpse of you from my vestry and I said, No, it's not him, it can't be. But of course, who else could it be looking so handsome and imposing. Your prayers are answered, I said to myself, your prayers are answered, you doubting Thomas. And how is the little lady, the courageous one who kept the fort in the absence of brother and father? Overjoyed, I am sure, overjoyed. So are we all.

He observes nothing of BERO's *cold attitude nor the fact that* BERO *has moved casually away from the patronizing arm which he tried to place on his shoulder.*

I meant to call on one or two neighbours on the way but that's just the selfish sinner I am, may God forgive me. No, I decided, I'll just have him all to myself for a little bit.

BERO. That's rather lucky.

PRIEST. Beg your pardon?

SI BERO. He's tired, Pastor. Don't let it out he's back yet.

PRIEST. Of course not. I wouldn't dream of doing such a thing. We all have our human failings of course, but I do know how inconsiderate people can be in their joys. Wouldn't think a man who's just returned from the seventh outpost of hell would want a little time to himself. I've suffered from my old complaint, you know, my boy, but I can suffer a little longer. Just get settled, son, just get settled and give yourself a well-deserved rest.

SI BERO. Pastor, you know I offered you . . .

PRIEST. Not quite the same thing, young lady, not quite the same thing. The doctor used to make those extracts with his own hand and . . .

SI BERO. It was the same one he made before he left.

PRIEST. No no, I could tell the difference. Oh yes, I could tell.

SI BERO. It was the same.

PRIEST. Good of you to try, but no. You just didn't make it the same. I could tell the difference at once. As soon as you're rested, my boy, as soon as you've rested . . . oh dear me. How shameful. Here I am complaining of my little fits and I haven't even asked news of my good friend. When is your father coming, my lad?

BERO. Soon.

SI BERO. Bero was just telling me . . .

PRIEST. Soon. How soon?

BERO. Soon enough.

PRIEST. Not soon enough for me, boy, not soon enough. I can't wait to take issue with him on all our old debates. Such an argumentative man, your father, such an argumentative man. And he'll have some stories to tell me, I'm sure. Really looking forward to our long evenings together. What an experience he must have had, what an experience! You know, it's strange how these disasters bring out the very best in man – and the worst sometimes. In your father's case, of course, the very best. Truly noble. I couldn't believe my ears when he got up one day and said he was going to join you. At your age, I said, you doddering old thing? I used to call him that, you know, and he would call me the mitred hypocrite. All in play, of course, only in play. So he . . . where was I? Something about your father, I believe. Oh yes, he suddenly got up one evening, right in the midst of our argument and said, I am going to see what's going on.

He was just reading me a letter from you and he got all worked up. It can't be, he shouted. And then he leapt up and said – right out of the blue – we've got to legalize cannibalism. Yes, right out of the blue. What do you mean, I said, thinking he only wanted to start another argument. But no, he repeats it over and over and of course, I took him on. Legalize cannibalism? It's a damnable and heathenish idea. Yes, that's how we started the argument. Warmest session we ever had together. He wouldn't yield one foot and I wouldn't budge one inch. Not one fraction of an inch. My polemical spirit was aroused. Not to talk of Christian principles. For three hours I fought him foot by foot. Never been in better form. Nearly all night we argued, if you please, and then in the morning he was gone. What do you make of that?

SI BERO. Pastor, I think Bero is a little tired . . .

PRIEST. Had only one letter from him all that time. Told me he was doing recuperative work among some disabled fellows. No forwarding address, if you please. I couldn't even continue our old debate by post. Strange man, your father, very strange. You didn't run into him out there, did you? I'm really anxious to know if he still intends to legalize cannibalism.

BERO. He does.

PRIEST. I knew it. A stubborn man, once he gets hold of an idea. You won't believe it but he actually said to me, I'm going to try and persuade those fools not to waste all that meat. Mind you he never could stand wastage, could he? I remember he used to wade into you both if he caught you wasting anything. But human flesh, why, that's another matter altogether.

BERO. But why, Pastor. It's quite delicious, you know.

PRIEST. Just what I say. It's . . . what did you say?

BERO (*reaches out and pulls out the* PRIEST's *cheek*). This. Delicious.

PRIEST (*struggles free*). You're joking, of course.

BERO. No. Your friend will confirm it when he comes.

PRIEST (*increasingly horrified*). You mean he . . .

BERO. No, not him. He never meant anything. At least, not that way. But we found it delicious just the same.

PRIEST. You?

BERO. I give you the personal word of a scientist. Human flesh is delicious. Of course, not all parts of the body. I prefer the balls myself.

PRIEST (*vehemently*). I don't believe you.

BERO. You don't? Well, then, why don't you stay to dinner?

PRIEST. Dinner? (*Cheering up.*) Of course. I see all you want is an argument like your old man. Delighted, of course. Only too delighted to oblige . . . (*He is stricken by a sudden doubt.*) Er . . . dinner . . . did you say dinner?

BERO. Dinner. I came well-laden with supplies.

The PRIEST *glances at* BERO's *bulging briefcase lying near by, gulps.*

PRIEST. I . . . er . . . I am wondering if I haven't got a little christening to attend to. I . . . er . . . couldn't simply come for drinks afterwards?

BERO. A christening so late in the evening?

PRIEST. Well, you know, the blessing at home and all that. The christening was this morning. (*He is already retreating.*) God bless you, my children both. I shall hurry back as soon as it's all over. Can't get rid of these extra parish duties . . . welcome back once again, my boy . . .

They watch him take flight.

SI BERO (*laughing*). You know, for a moment I nearly believed you.

BERO. Oh? (*Turns and looks at her pityingly.*) You didn't?

Pause. The look each other in the face. Her laughter dies slowly.

SI BERO. Oh God.

BERO. Out of your world, little sister, out of your little world. Stay in it and do only what I tell you. That way you'll be safe.

SI BERO (*vehemently*). Abomination!

BERO. Delicious, you heard me say.

SI BERO. Abomination!

BERO (*deliberate cruelty*). Delicious. The balls, to be exact. I thought I told you to stay in your little world! Go and take tea with the senile pastor or gossip with your old women. Don't come out from where you're safe. (*Quietly.*) Or sane.

SI BERO. But at least tell me why? In God's name why?

BERO. No, not in God's name – in the name of As!

SI BERO. What?

BERO. As. The new god and the old – As.

SI BERO. What are you trying to be, Bero – evil?

BERO. Does it sound that bad? It was no brain-child of mine. We thought it was a joke. I'll bless the meat, he said. And then – As Was the Beginning, As is, Now, As Ever shall be . . . world without. . . . We said amen with a straight face and sat down to eat. Then, afterwards . . .

SI BERO. Yes?

BERO. He told us. (*Pause. He laughs suddenly.*) But why not? Afterwards I said why not? What is one flesh from another? So I tried it again, just to be sure of myself. It was the first step to power you understand. Power in its purest sense. The end of inhibitions. The conquest of the weakness of your too human flesh with all its sentiment. So again, all to myself I said Amen to his grace.

SI BERO. I don't follow you, Bero. Who said grace? Whose words are these?

BERO. Father's part of the liturgy of his bed-ridden audience. Wait a minute. (*Pointing to the* MENDICANTS.) They can tell you more about it.

SI BERO. Who? These? What they have to do with . . .?

BERO. Have you never thought how they came to beg so close to here? At the beginning, that is. Before I found out about them.

SI BERO. Oh, is that it? You mean he sent them? But you know him – Liberty House. It's not a crime. I found them work to do.

BERO (*heatedly*). It's not his charitable propensities I am concerned with. Father's assignment was to help the wounded readjust to the pieces and remnants of their bodies. Physically. Teach them to make baskets if they still had fingers. To use their mouths to ply needles if they had none, or use it to sing if their vocal cords had not been shot away. Teach them to amuse themselves, make something of themselves. Instead he began to teach them to think, think, THINK! Can you picture a more treacherous deed than to place a working mind in a mangled body?

SI BERO. Where is he?

BERO. Where? Here.

SI BERO. Here?

BERO (*pointing to the* MENDICANTS). There. When they open their mouths you can hear him. You! Come here! Tell her. Would you call yourself sane?

The MENDICANTS *have approached,* AAFAA *in the lead.*

AAFAA. Certainly not, sir.

BERO. You got off lightly, Why?

AAFAA. I pleaded insanity.

BERO. Who made you insane?

AAFAA (*by rote, raising his eyes to heaven*). The Old Man, sir. He said things, he said things. My mind . . . I beg your pardon, sir, the thing I call my mind, well, was no longer there. He took advantage of me, sir, in that convalescent home. I was unconscious long stretches at a time. Whatever I saw when I came to was real. Whatever voice I heard was the truth. It was always him. Bending over my bed. I asked him, Who are you? He answered, The one and only truth.

CRIPPLE. Hear hear.

GOYI. Same here.

AAFAA. Always at me, he was, sir. I plead insanity.

CRIPPLE. Hear hear.

GOYI. Same here.

AAFAA (*pointing to* BLINDMAN). Even him.

BLINDMAN. Once I even thought I could see him.

GOYI. Oh, but you did, you did.

BLINDMAN. No, not really.

CRIPPLE. You did, you did. The picture forms in the mind, remember?

GOYI. His very words. But any fool knows they form on the eye.

AAFAA. Lord, he mixed us up.

BLINDMAN. You can see me, he said, you can see me. Look at me with your mind. I swear I began to see him. Then I knew I was insane.

CRIPPLE. Hear hear.

GOYI. Same here.

AAFAA. We all did.

CRIPPLE. And getting me all choosy!

BLINDMAN. Poor you.

CRIPPLE. Beggars can't be choosers, we all knew that.

AAFAA. Yet he got you choosy.

CRIPPLE. I was mad.

BLINDMAN (*changing his voice*). Remember, even if you have nothing left but your vermin, discriminate between one bug and the next.

CRIPPLE. Some bugs are friendly, others wild.

GOYI. The one sucks gently, the other nips.

BLINDMAN. If you must eat a toad . . .

CRIPPLE. . . . pick the fat one, with eggs in its belly.

AAFAA. Listen to the fool. It's you he's calling a toad.

The CRIPPLE *advances on him.*

GOYI. No, it wasn't. Don't listen to him.

AAFAA (*voice change*). You'll listen now or you'll listen later!

SI BERO. Where is Father?

AAFAA. Where is he, where is he? As is everywhere.

CRIPPLE (*picking a flea from his rags*). Got him!

SI BERO (*turning sharply*). What!

CRIPPLE (*throwing it in his mouth*). A fat one.

GOYI. Greedy beggar.

AAFAA. Did you choose it?

CRIPPLE. It chose me.

BLINDMAN. Chose? An enemy of As.

AAFAA. Sure? Not a disciple.

BLINDMAN. An enemy. Subversive agent.

AAFAA. Quite right. As chooses, man accepts. Had it sucked any blood?

CRIPPLE. It tasted bloody.

GOYI. Accept my sympathies.

CRIPPLE. Not needed. The blood is back where it belongs.

AAFAA. The cycle is complete?

CRIPPLE. Definitely.

GOYI. Then you can't complain.

SI BERO. What is this, Bero? Where is Father?

AAFAA. Within the cycle.

BLINDMAN. That's good. The cycle of As. Tell the Old Man that – he'll be pleased.

SI BERO. Where is he?

AAFAA. Where the cycle is complete there will As be found. As of the beginning, we praise thee.

SI BERO (*shutting her ears*). Oh God!

BERO (*pointing to the* MENDICANTS). Do you still want to see him?

AAFAA. As – Was – Is – Now.

SI BERO. Shut up, you loathsome toads!

There is a brief silence. They all look at her.

AAFAA (*grinning*). Toads again. You hear that?

CRIPPLE. She was looking at you.

AAFAA. What! I must say I feel insulted.

CRIPPLE. A man must have some pride.

GOYI. My pride is – As.

AAFAA. And all in the line of duty. Sir, I demand protection.

BERO. That's enough. Open the surgery. (*He turns to* SI BERO.)
You want to see him? You shall.

MENDICANTS (*already moving towards the surgery*). As – Was
– Is – Now – As Ever Shall Be . . .
Bi o ti wa
Ni yio se wa
Bi o ti wa
Ni yio se wa
Bi o ti wa l'atete ko se . . .

SI BERO. And what in God's name is that?

BERO. One of their chants. (*He grabs her arm as she tries to run
after the* MENDICANTS.) Now listen, and always remember
this – he is wholly in my charge.

SI BERO. How long? How long has he been home?

BERO. Home? What home? I tell you he is here in my charge. It
was either this or . . . Do not interfere!

*He holds her with his eyes for a few moments, then moves to
follow the* MENDICANTS. *He stops when he sees that she
has made no attempt to follow.*

You want to see him? Come on.

Pause. SI BERO *looks at him with increasing horror and dis-
belief. She turns and runs towards the* OLD WOMEN *who
receive her at the door of the hut.* BERO *goes on into the clinic
where the light has come on, revealing the* OLD MAN *seated
in the midst of the chanting* MENDICANTS. *Lights fade
slowly.*

Part Two

The surgery, below the ground floor of the house. An examination couch, assortment of a few instruments and jars in a locked glass case, a chromium sterilizing unit etc. etc., a table, swivel chair etc., a white smock hangs against a shelf, with surgical mask and gloves tucked in the pockets. The MENDICANTS *are crouched, standing, stooping in their normal postures, humming their chant and listlessly throwing dice. The* OLD MAN'S *attitude varies from boredom to tolerant amusement.*

AAFAA. A. As is Acceptance, Adjustment. Adjustment of Ego to the Acceptance of As . . . hm. Not bad. B . . . B . . . . (*His eye roams over the room for inspiration, falls on the* BLIND-MAN.) Of course. B, Blindness. Blindness in As. I say this unto you, As is all-seeing; All shall see in As who render themselves blind to all else. C . . . C? (*He looks at the others one by one but ends up shaking his head.*) No, nothing from you lot this time. Can't see how I can ask the flock to get crippled for some reward in As. C . . . No, I'll have to skip it for now. D – good – I don't have to go far for that. D, Divinity. That's us. For Destiny too. In fact Destiny first, then Divinity. Destiny is the Duty of Divinity. D-D-D – Destiny in 3-Dimension. We the Divinity shall guide the flock along the path of Destiny. E . . .

BLINDMAN. Epilepsy?

AAFAA (*sharply*). Watch your mouth!

BLINDMAN. For your Divinity to have control, the flock must be without control. Epilepsy seems to be the commonest form – at least, I have witnessed much that is similar.

GOYI. I know what you mean. Taken by the spirit, they call it. It's a good circus turn any day. Aafaa should know.

AAFAA. You are not suggesting I exploited human infirmities, are you?

CRIPPLE. I wish I had the power. Gives a man a sense of power to watch others twitch like so many broken worms. Broken worms, ah, that's a fine thing to come from my mouth.

AAFAA. Before we get to Z I promise you your private and personal consolation. F . . . F . . . F . . .

GOYI. As farts, damn you! (*He turns his rear and gestures obscenely.*)

AAFAA. I was going to suggest Fulfils. As fulfils.

GOYI. And I say Farts.

AAFAA. Are you going to confront your Destiny with a fart?

GOYI. I have done before. I did it in that place where they treated us. Treatment! No doctor. Only nurses who couldn't tell a man's end from their own. Hey, listen, and let me tell you, it was the cleverest thing I ever thought all those sweet times we spent with the Old Man. With him saying this and saying that to us and me on my side – couldn't turn on my back and couldn't turn on my belly – and the sun would come up one day and I wouldn't see it again until it come up the next. One time he told us – remember that day? – he told us the earth goes round and round, which if you remember was just too much for someone like me to swallow. So, the following morning when the sun came round again, I said to myself, well, I suppose the Old Man must be right. I don't know what makes the world go round but I do know what goes round the world. It's wind. And I broke it loudly and felt better.

CRIPPLE. Dirty pig.

GOYI. It's all very well for you to talk. You could get around even then. I sometimes think God made you out of rubber or something.

AAFAA (*who has been thinking his own thoughts, gives a sudden shout*). God, that's it. Godhead! What a real pagan I've become if that took me so long. G, As is Godhead. I is next.

BLINDMAN. I am I, what more do you want?

AAFAA (*chews it over*). I am I, thus sayeth As. No . . . that might cause trouble.

BLINDMAN. What kind of trouble?

AAFAA. Think of it yourself. Sooner or later someone is going to say it and leave out 'so sayeth As'. And that means trouble.

GOYI. I don't follow.

CRIPPLE. Ask the Old Man. He'll settle the question.

They turn towards the OLD MAN, *but he is still motionless, unresponsive.*

AAFAA. Old Man, what do you think of the I matter?

Again they wait in vain for his response.

All right, if that doesn't interest you, at least give us something between I and Z. That is still a long way to go and already I can feel my brain giving out. Not to talk of the others. Anything you like, your forgotten wishes, your deepest cravings, your pet dreams . . .

GOYI. S-sh!

CRIPPLE. Why do you keep making fun of him? Leave him alone.

AAFAA (*looks genuinely surprised*). But I . . .

GOYI. That's what he used to say. You were using his very words just to mock him.

AAFAA. Well, I didn't mean to.

His apparent contrition leaves the others a little flat. They steal furtive glances at the OLD MAN *who does not move.*

CRIPPLE. I have a pet dream.

AAFAA. We know what that is, so shut up!

BLINDMAN. I want to hear his pet dream.

AAFAA. Can't you guess what it is by seeing where he scratches himself at night?

BLINDMAN. No, I cannot see.

A brief pause.

CRIPPLE. I'll tell you. Every night we sleep in this place I have that same dream. It's what makes me stay on. It is what makes me . . . assist . . .

AAFAA. Collaborate.

CRIPPLE. I don't know what the big word means.

BLINDMAN (*gently*). No. Don't bother with it. Continue with your dream.

CRIPPLE. It is what makes me continue to obey the specialist.

Pause.

OLD MAN (*unnoticed, he has turned round to face them*). Go on, your dream.

CRIPPLE (*for a moment he, with the rest, shows confusion*). I . . . dream he tells me to get on that table. He says, I could not attend to you before but there were other things . . . one thing at a time, certain things are more important than others. So he operates on my back and in another moment he's finished, wipes his hands and says . . .

AAFAA. Arise, throw off thy crutches and follow me.

CRIPPLE (*lowering his eyes as if in abashment*). Yes, more or less the same words. But just as I want to get up, I wake up from the blasted dream!

AAFAA (*with explosive disgust*). That's a permanent dream if ever I heard one. You think the specialist has time for your petty little inconvenience? You're getting to be quite important in your mind to afford dreams like that. I wouldn't dare. Would you? (*Turning to* GOYI. *The* CRIPPLE *turns his head in confusion.*) Oh, you too? What have we here? A conspiracy of the élite? I suppose you too have been dreaming you'll get back your sight from him? No, I should have known you better. Just these two. (*Explosively.*) You are just the kind of people who make life impossible for professionals. Miracle, Miracle! That's all we ever get out of your smelly mouths. Because you blackmailed one Christ into showing off once in a while you think all others are suckers for that kind of showmanship. Well, you've met your match this generation. Turn left, turn right, turn right about again, you'll find everyone you meet is more than a match for you.

A short pause.

BLINDMAN. Isn't it time for his food?

AAFAA. The little woman will knock when it's ready. And let him starve a bit anyway, why not? He got us into this mess. If there is one thing I can't stand it's amateurs. Even there I didn't like him all that much. Now the specialist – that's a professional. You only need to remember it's father and son. Human beings both of them. Who is my neighbour, you know – all that stuff and sentiment.

A knock on the door. They all fall silent. The three seeing MENDICANTS *dart a look at the* OLD MAN. *The knock is repeated.*

All right, we heard. Put down the tray and go back to your hole. Go on. Get going.

They listen to the footsteps retreat out of hearing.

(*He chants at the* OLD MAN.) Lord, now lettest thou thy servant depart in peace, according to thy word. (*To* BLINDMAN.) Are you going to open the door?

BLINDMAN *sighs, gets up, followed by* GOYI. *He unbolts the door and* GOYI *exits. He bolts it again,* AAFAA *watching every movement.*

Chop time, Old Man. Your food is on the way.

OLD MAN. Did you take my watch? (*He stirs and feels in his breast pocket.*)

AAFAA. It was broken. I sent it for repairs.

OLD MAN. You have it on your wrist.

AAFAA. Mistaken identity. (*Holding up his wrist.*) Take a look if you like.

OLD MAN. You took my glasses also.

AAFAA (*dips into his pocket*). Try these. No? They might just fit you never can tell. They used to belong to him. (*Pointing to* BLINDMAN.) Are you sure you wouldn't try them? After the blast took off his eyes – that's how we first met – it was my job to go round comforting the poor fools – or burying them. Anyway – and that's the strange thing; the glasses were knocked off all right, but not a scratch on them. So he says, take my glasses from that bedside cupboard in case someone else needs them. I've kept them ever since. Are you sure you won't try them?

OLD MAN. Let me see that watch again.

AAFAA. It won't tell you anything.

OLD MAN. Which of you took my glasses?

AAFAA. What does it matter?

OLD MAN. I want to see what's in the food. What are you giving me to eat?

AAFAA. Leave that to us.

A sudden peremptory knock on the door. Enter BERO, *followed by* GOYI *bearing a tray of food.*

BERO. I thought I would join you for dinner.

OLD MAN (*rounding on him*). Will you tell me just what is going on?

BERO. Nothing Old Man, nothing.

OLD MAN. I wish to write a letter.

BERO. Who to?

OLD MAN. To your superiors.

BERO (*winces, but recovers his poise*). There isn't such a thing.

OLD MAN. Your superiors, I said. I demand the right to send to them at once.

Pause. Finally.

BERO. You shall.

OLD MAN. I wish to write them at once. Now!

BERO (*turns to* AAFAA). Fetch some writing material. Go to the nearest stationers.

OLD MAN. Why all the way to look for a store? Isn't there any in the house?

BERO. None that belongs to you. Perhaps you would give him money for your requirements?

> The OLD MAN *starts to take money from his pockets, slows down in suspicion and looks at* BERO. *Then, slowly, he dips into all his trouser pockets.*

OLD MAN. You know you took my money. Or ordered it removed.

BERO. I don't know anything of the sort.

OLD MAN (*violently*). You know I have no money here!

BERO. I don't know anything. You on the contrary appear to know everything. Isn't that right? You know everything. (*To* AAFAA.) The Old Man appears to have no money. Obviously he can have no writing paper. Perhaps you would like to send a verbal message?

OLD MAN. You can take your verbal message to – (*He looks at him scornfully, then sits down.*)

BERO. I tried to help. You will, of course, be given the best of everything you need. Need. (*Pause.*) Your food will get cold.

OLD MAN. I need my pipe.

BERO (*appears to consider it*). Why not? In this case I raise my idea of your need to coincide with your want.

> *He opens a cabinet, gives him his pipe and tobacco.*

That gentleman there will offer you a light whenever you – need it.

> *The* OLD MAN *begins to stuff his pipe, normally at first, then slower and slower. When the pipe is filled he holds it*

by the bowl, waiting. AAFAA *dips his hand in his pocket as if about to pull out matches, pauses, slowly holds out a closed fist then opens it suddenly to reveal the hand empty. He breaks into silent laughter.*

OLD MAN. I need a light.

BERO. And your watch. And glasses. And money. And paper. But do you really? I promised you the best of everything and this will prove to you I mean it. (*He takes a packet of cigarettes from his pocket and offers it.*) They are the best cigarettes on the market.

He takes out a packet of matches, holds out both matches and cigarettes in one hand, holds out the other hand, inviting him to return the pipe and tobacco.

OLD MAN. I prefer . . . my pipe.

BERO *does not move. A long pause. The* OLD MAN *looks round at the* MENDICANTS *avidly watching. Finally he returns the pipe and pouch, accepts the cigarettes and matches, but moves the packet against his face to read the brand name.*

BERO. You can't see to read.

The OLD MAN *snatches the box away from his face, opens the box and takes out a cigarette, lights it, then breaks into a slow smile.*

OLD MAN. You would, wouldn't you? You would try that on me. Me! Shall I teach you what to say? Choice! Particularity! What redundant self-deceptive notions! More? More? Insistence on a floppy old coat, a rickety old chair, a moth-eaten hat which no certified lunatic would ever consider wearing, a car which breaks down twenty times in twenty minutes, an old idea riddled with the pellets of incidence. Enough? More? Are you cramming it up fast for the next victim? A perfect waterproof coat is rejected for a patched-up heirloom that gives the silly wearer rheumatism. Is this an argument for freedom of choice? Is it sensible to cling so desperately to bits of the bitter end of a run-down personality? To the creak in an old chair, the crack in a cup, a crock of an old servant, the crick in the bottleneck of a man's declining years . . . (*Pause. His voice changes.*) But it did come to the test and I asked you all, what is one meat from another? Oh, your faces then, your faces . . .

BERO. You still boast of that? You go too far, Old Man.

OLD MAN. After all, what's meat for the ranks should be meat for the officers . . . (*Chuckles.*) It could happen I said, it will happen. But I never really believed it.

BERO. They would have killed you, you know that? If I hadn't had you hidden away they would have killed you slowly.

OLD MAN (*still on his own*). No. I've asked myself over and over again. I said it would happen, I knew it would happen, but I never really believed it.

BERO. They wanted to kill you, mutilate you, hang you upside down then stuff your mouth with your own genitals. Did you know that? (*His explosiveness breaks in on the* OLD MAN.)

OLD MAN. Why do you hesitate?

BERO. To do what?

OLD MAN. I said, why do you hesitate? (*Pause.*) Once you begin there is no stopping. You say, ah, this is the last step, the highest step, but there is always one more step. For those who want to step beyond, there is always one further step.

BERO. Nothing more is needed.

OLD MAN. Oh yes, there is. I am the last proof of the human in you. The last shadow. Shadows are tough things to be rid of. (*He chuckles.*) How does one prove he was never born of man? Of course you could kill me . . .

BERO. Or you might just die . . .

OLD MAN. Quite possible, quite possible.

BERO. You're lucky you've lasted this far.

OLD MAN. I *have* lasted, but the question of being lucky . . .?

BERO. There is a search for you everywhere.

OLD MAN. I thought that was over. Tenacious gods they worship, don't they?

BERO. And you?

OLD MAN. Or maybe they are the tenacious gods.

BERO. And the god you worship?

OLD MAN. Abominates humanity – the fleshy part, that is.

BERO. Why As?

OLD MAN. Because Was – Is – Now . . .

BERO. Don't!

OLD MAN. So you see, I put you all beyond salvation.

BERO. Why As?

OLD MAN. A code. A word.

BERO. Why As?

OLD MAN. It had to be something.

BERO. Why As?

OLD MAN. If millions follow . . . that frightened you all.

BERO. Why As?

OLD MAN. Are you going to reopen the files? The case is closed. Insane, the verdict, thanks to you.

BERO. Why As?

OLD MAN. Why not?

BERO. Why As?

OLD MAN. Who wants to know?

BERO. I. Why As?

OLD MAN. What's in it for you?

BERO. *I* am asking questions! Why As?

OLD MAN. We went through this before.

BERO. I took a chance saving you.

OLD MAN. Risked your neck, yes. Compromised your position.

BERO. I didn't do that for nothing.

OLD MAN. It won't be for nothing. As my next-in-line you are my beneficiary. Legal. These of course are my natural heirs.

BERO. To what?

OLD MAN. As. What else?

BERO. I could turn you out and let them find you.

OLD MAN. The file is closed.

BERO. Is it? They are still looking for you.

OLD MAN. They should be looking for themselves. I robbed them of salvation.

BERO. Oh yes, you are good at quibbling.

OLD MAN. Oh, their faces! That was a picture. All those faces round the table.

BERO. If they hadn't been too surprised they would have shot you on the spot.

OLD MAN. Your faces, gentlemen, your faces. You should see your faces. And your mouths are hanging open. You're drooling but I am not exactly sure why. Is there really much difference? All intelligent animals kill only for food, you know, and you are intelligent animals. Eat-eat-eat-eat-eat-Eat!

BERO (*raises his arm*). Stop it!

OLD MAN (*turns and holds him with his eyes*). Oh yes, you rushed out and vomited. You and the others. But afterwards you said I had done you a favour. Remember? (BERO *slowly lowers his arm.*) I'm glad you remember. Never admit you are a recidivist once you've tasted the favourite food of As.

Pause.

BERO. That's your last meal. Eat.

Going out.

OLD MAN. Because it's *your* last chance? (BERO *stops but doesn't turn round.*) I guessed it. You have to prove you have not yourself been contaminated. But suppose you find no answer to take back, what then? (*Pause, smiling.*) The – choice – is simple. *Be* contaminated!

BERO *exits, slamming the door.*

AAFFA (*dashes towards the food tray, opens the lid and sniffs*).
Inspiration! C, Contentment. A full belly. (*He starts to pick
at the* OLD MAN's *food. The others join him, wolfing down huge
chunks of meat.* AAFAA *gnaws at a huge bone.*) A full belly
comes and goes; for half the people I know it never comes.
H – Humanity! Humanity the Ultimate Sacrifice to As, the
eternal oblation on the altar of As . . . I say, I get better all
the time!

GOYI (*irritated*). At what? You're just a parrot.

AAFAA. I take exception to that. I'm a good pupil. The Old
Man himself admits it. The quickest of the underdogs, he
always said.

GOYI. Yes, underdogs. First the Old Man tells us we are the
underdogs, then his blasted son makes us his watchdogs!

AAFAA (*shrugs*). Makes life a little more amusing you'll
admit . . .

    They continue to eat.

BERO *and* SI BERO *meet in front of the house.*

BERO. What is it? Are you spying on me?

SI BERO. What are you doing to him?

BERO. Keeping him safe. What do you imagine?

SI BERO. I wish to see him.

BERO. I've told you already . . .

SI BERO. I wish to see him.

BERO. You had your chance. No one can see him now.

SI BERO. Why not?

BERO. He's dangerous.

SI BERO. I'll risk it.

BERO. Infectious diseases are isolated. Nothing unusual about
it, so stop making a fuss. I need to work in peace.

SI BERO. What am I to do? I have time on my hands. What can I do but think!

BERO. I've told you, leave the thinking to me. Stay in your little world and continue the work I set you.

SI BERO. That's over. And the old women no longer help. They sit and fold their arms.

BERO. I have no need of them. And you should never have brought them here. Throw them out.

SI BERO. They demand payment.

BERO. Then pay them off.

SI BERO. They won't take money.

BERO. So what do they want?

SI BERO. Nothing. But they refuse to leave until they are paid.

BERO (*looking in that direction*). They are asking for death.

SI BERO. They don't seem to be afraid of you, Bero.

BERO. We shall see.

He turns to go towards the hut.

SI BERO. Wait, Bero, wait!

BERO. Well?

SI BERO. Don't harm them, Bero.

BERO. Either you throw them out or I will. Whose home is it? Theirs? Do they now lay claim to the land?

SI BERO. It belongs to Father.

BERO. Forfeited. Legally, he does not exist. (*He goes into the house.*)

The surgery. The MENDICANTS *are picking at the last crumbs of food, licking the last bone of its meat. One or two are humming the 'Ballad of the Disabled'. The* OLD MAN *reacts to the sound of singing, listens, then turns away in disgust.*

OLD MAN. I should have known better.

AAFAA (*stops*). What, Old Man?

OLD MAN. For a moment I would have sworn I heard singing.

AAFAA. You heard us.

OLD MAN. I said singing, not cursing.

AAFAA. Perhaps you heard my spasms tuning up. It's like a set
of wires Old Man. Something touches them, they hum, and
off I go.

OLD MAN. It doesn't bother you much these days, I notice.

AAFAA. That's true. They told me up there when it began, that
it was something psy-cho-lo-gi-cal. Something to do with all
the things happening around me, and the narrow escape I
had. It's not so bad now. I still remember the first time. I
was standing there just like this, blessing a group of six
just about to go off. They were kneeling before me. Then –
well, I can't say I heard the noise at all, because I was deaf
for the next hour. So, this thing happened, no signal, no
nothing. Six men kneeling in front of me, the next moment
they were gone. Disappeared, just like that. That was when
I began to shake. Nothing I could do to stop it. My back just
went on bending over and snapping back again, like the
spirit had taken me. God! What a way for the spirit to mount
a man.

OLD MAN. But no revelations? No inspired pronouncements?

AAFAA (angrily). What of you! I don't see you saving yourself
in the situation you're in. (More to himself.) Or us.

OLD MAN. There is nothing you can do, of course.

GOYI. Be fair Old Man, how does a man cope with a situation
like this? It was all right in the other place.

OLD MAN. So you find it different from the other places?

GOYI. It's not the same.

OLD MAN. There was no madness – then? (They react, silently.)
You were not maimed then? (He holds up his hand to stop
them.) And I mean, not merely in body. You were maimed
then as now. You have lost the gift of self-disgust.

AAFAA. So have you, Old Man.

OLD MAN. Meaning?

CRIPPLE. I know what he means. I agree with him.

GOYI. So do I.

OLD MAN (*smiling*). Explain. I do not understand.

CRIPPLE. You took the cigarette.

AAFAA. A man like me is letting himself down to say he is surprised by anything, but . . . I was surprised at you, Old Man. You may say I was a bit let down. We may be on opposite sides of the camp, but I like to see a man stand up for himself.

OLD MAN. Why?

AAFAA. So I can beat him down.

He guffaws but no one joins him. He subsides.

OLD MAN. You were disgusted?

AAFAA (*soberly*). More than.

The OLD MAN *turns silently to each of them in turn.*

CRIPPLE. Disappointed.

GOYI. Crucified.

OLD MAN. Disgust is cheap. I asked for self-disgust.

AAFAA. Yeah? You took the cigarette – what about that?

OLD MAN. Of course I did. Because I saw your faces.

He reaches in his pocket and throws towards them what turns out to be the barely smoked cigarette. All three pounce on it; the CRIPPLE *comes out the winner.*

AAFAA. Only one puff, only one and then you pass it round.

OLD MAN (*watches them with contempt*). We'll go on that world tour yet. I'll take your circus round the world, so help me.

CRIPPLE (*slowly releasing a puff of smoke*). Oh, that feels good. Haven't had such a good puff since that corpulent First Lady visited us and passed round imported cigarettes.

GOYI. The Old Man was mad for days. Suckers, he called us. Quite right too. Good smoke is a good suck. I wasn't going to throw away that superior brand just to please a crackpot.

AAFAA. Hey, remember the song the Old Man wrote to celebrate the occasion? Visit of the First Lady to the Home
for the de-balled.

BLINDMAN. . . . for the Disabled.

AAFAA. Bloody pendant.

BLINDMAN. Pe-dant.

AAFAA (*gives up*). Oh Christ!

CRIPPLE (*singing*).
   He came smelling of wine and roses, wine and roses

MENDICANTS.   . . . wine and roses.

 AAFAA *gradually warms up towards his spastic dance.*

CRIPPLE. He came smelling of wine and roses.
   On his arm his wife was gushpillating . . .

BLINDMAN. Palpitating.

AAFAA. Oh, can't you shut up? Don't mind him, start all over
again.

CRIPPLE. He came smelling of wine and roses.
   On his arm his wife was gushpillating, gushpillating . . .

MENDICANTS.   . . . gushpillating.

 The singing fades out.
 BERO *comes out of the house, holstering a revolver. He goes
 up to the* OLD WOMEN's *hut quietly and tries to peep inside.*
 IYA AGBA *leans out of the hut and speaks almost directly
 in his ear.*

IYA AGBA. Does the specialist have time for a word or two?

 BERO *is startled, leaps aside.*

Did I scare you?

BERO (*recovering, looks her over carefully*). What is a thing like
you still doing alive?

IYA AGBA. Can we help you?

BERO. Do what? Just pack up and get out of here before morning.

IYA AGBA. We can help you cure him.

BERO. Who?

IYA AGBA. He's sick, that is what we heard.

BERO. You heard wrong. I am giving you warning to clear out of here. Pick up your lice and rags and get out.

IYA AGBA. Is anyone else sick that we know of?

BERO. By tomorrow I want you out.

IYA AGBA. We want to help him.

BERO. No one needs help from you. Now get out of my way.

IYA AGBA. Maybe you do.

BERO. Do I have to fling you aside!

IYA AGBA (*stands aside*). Pass, then.

She lets him take a few steps, then.

Your sister owes us a debt.

BERO (*stops, turns slowly*). If you know what is good for you, you will never let me hear that again.

IYA AGBA. We took her into the fold – did she tell you that? To teach what we know, a pupil must come into the fold.

BERO. What fold? Some filthy thieving cult?

IYA AGBA. It's no light step for man or woman.

BERO. And what . . . cult is this?

IYA AGBA. Not any cult you can destroy. We move as the Earth moves, nothing more. We age as Earth ages.

BERO. But you're afraid to tell me the name.

IYA AGBA. I try to keep fools from temptation.

BERO (*instantly angry*). Watch it, old woman, your age earns no privileges with me.

IYA AGBA. Nothing does from what we hear. So you want to know what cult, do you?

BERO. I can ask your – pupil.

He turns round to go back to his house.

IYA AGBA. She won't tell you. Take it from me. She won't.

> BERO *stops without turning, waits.*

Your mind has run farther than the truth. I see it searching, going round and round in darkness. Truth is always too simple for a desperate mind.

BERO (*going*). I shall find out.

IYA AGBA. Don't look for the sign of broken bodies or wandering souls. Don't look for the sound of fear or the smell of hate. Don't take a bloodhound with you; we don't mutilate bodies.

BERO. Don't teach me my business.

IYA AGBA. If you do, you may find him circle back to your door.

BERO. Watch your mouth, old hag.

IYA AGBA. You want the name? But how much would it tell you, young man? We put back what we take, in one form or another. Or more than we take. It's the only law. What laws do you obey?

BERO. You are proscribed, whatever you are, you are banned.

IYA AGBA. What can that mean? You'll proscribe Earth itself? How does one do that?

BERO. I offer you a last chance.

IYA AGBA. The fool is still looking for names. How much would it tell you?

BERO. You'll find out when they come for you.

IYA AGBA. What will you step on young fool? Even on the road to damnation a man must rest his foot somewhere.

> BERO *marches furiously back to the surgery. He is stopped at the door by the sound coming from the surgery. He listens.*

CRIPPLE. . . . On his arm his wife was gushpillating, gushpillating . . .

MENDICANTS.   . . . gushpillating . . .

CRIPPLE. You never saw such a gushpillating wife
        Oh, was it gross and was it ugly, was it ugly . . .

MENDICANTS.   . . . was it ugly . . .

CRIPPLE. That thing he had clinging onto his arm
        And she knew that all the men did think so, men did
        think so . . .

MENDICANTS.   . . . men did think so . . .

CRIPPLE. Did find their own predicaments much prettier.
        So she looked them mean and smiled them dirty,
        smiled them dirty . . .

MENDICANTS.   . . . smiled them dirty . . .

CRIPPLE. And her mouth formed silent words
        I may be gross but dears, I'm not beyond it, not
        beyond it . . .

MENDICANTS.   . . . not beyond it . . .

CRIPPLE. I may be old but not beyond it.
        While you according to diagnosis, diagnosis . . .

MENDICANTS.   . . . diagnosis . . .

CRIPPLE. Will ne . . . ver . . .

*He pauses, splutters as if trying to control his mirth, which
finally breaks out fully. The* MENDICANTS *join in, then at a
rallying signal from* AAFAA, *control themselves long enough
to end –*

ALL. . . . hm-hm-hm . . . no more.

AAFAA. That was the best song you ever wrote for us, Old Man.
  Ballad of the State Visit to the Home of the De-balled.

CRIPPLE. I prefer the second one.

GOYI. Which one?

CRIPPLE. Pro patria mourir.

MENDICANTS. . . . mourir mourir mourir . . .

CRIPPLE. Dulce et decorum . . .

MENDICANTS. . . . quorum quorum quorum . . .

OLD MAN. Corum, stupes, not quorum.

MENDICANTS. Corum corum corum, not quorum.

OLD MAN. Decorum. Dulce et decorum . . .

MENDICANTS. . . . quorum quorum quorum . . .

OLD MAN. God damn you. Can you learn nothing? – corum, not quorum.

GOYI. No quorum, no quorum, that's the damned trouble.

CRIPPLE. Yes sir, you've banged the hammer on the nail.

OLD MAN (*turning to* AAFAA). Will you tell me what these idiots are talking about?

AAFAA. They've lost me.

CRIPPLE. You've gone dense. (*Quoting the* OLD MAN *again.*) In ancient Athens . . .

AAFAA. Damn it, you're right. No damned quorum!

BLINDMAN. In ancient Athens they didn't just have a quorum. Everybody was there! That, children, was democracy.

CRIPPLE (*singing, to the tune of 'When the Saints'*).

Before I join
The saints above
Before I join
The saints above
I want to sit on that damned quorum
Before I join the saints above

Before I bid
This earth adieu
Before I bid
This earth adieu
I want my dues from that damned quorum
Before I bid this earth adieu

> *The others join in, drumming on the floor, table, etc., with their crutches, knuckles, etc., repeating the chorus. 'I want my dues . . . Before adieus' in place of 'Oh when the Saints . . . Go marching in'.*
>
> *As the tempo warms up* BERO *enters.*

BERO (*entering*). So you haven't given up your little tricks.

OLD MAN. Does it bother you?

BERO. No. It is bad for you, though.

OLD MAN. It seems to interest you. Spend more time with us.

BERO. What gives you that idea?

OLD MAN. I could hear you listening outside. You were fascinated.

BERO. My interest in you is strictly . . .

OLD MAN. That of a specialist. Proceed.

BERO. How did you do it?

OLD MAN. Do what?

BERO. No more evasions. How did you do it? What made you do it?

OLD MAN. Prod. Prod. Probe. Probe. Don't you know yet what I am? (*Dramatic whisper.*) Octopus. Plenty of reach but nothing to seize on. I re-create my tentacles, so cut away.

BERO. To me you are simply another organism, another mould or strain under the lens. Sometimes a strain proves malignant and it becomes dangerous to continue with it. In such a case there is only one thing to do.

OLD MAN. Are you equipped for that here?

BERO. Even I have no control over accidents. Just now I came through that room of herbs, I saw something I recognized.

OLD MAN. Something to sap the mind? Or destroy it altogether?

BERO. It depends on the dose. I brought you some. (*He brings some berries from his pockets and drops them gently over the* OLD MAN's *head.*) If you ever get tired and you feel you need a nightcap like a certain ancient Greek you were so fond of quoting, just soak a handful of them in water.

OLD MAN. You've used it before, haven't you? Or something similar. I saw your victims, afterwards.

BERO. They were provided a Creed but they talked heresy. Same as you.

OLD MAN. Creed? Heresy? Bread, pleurisy and what next? Will you try and speak some intelligible language.

BERO. They corrupted unformed minds. That was ba-a-ad.

OLD MAN. Unformed minds in deformed bodies.

BERO. Again you are being evasive.

OLD MAN. I asked to be sent where I would do the most good. I was and I did.

BERO (*smiling*). I also was sent where I would do the most good. I was and I did. (*Pause.*) It would appear that we were both efficient volunteers. (*Again, pause.*) What exactly is As, Old Man?

OLD MAN. As?

BERO. You know As, the playword of your convalescents, the pivot of whatever doctrine you used to confuse their minds, your piffling battering ram at the idealism and purpose of this time and history. What is As, Old Man?

OLD MAN. You seem to have described it to your satisfaction.

BERO (*thundering. Moving suddenly, he passes his swagger-stick across the* OLD MAN's *throat, holding it from behind and pressing*). I'm asking you! What is As? Why As!

OLD MAN (*gasps but tries to smile. He cranes up to look him in the face*). In a way I should be flattered. You want to borrow my magic key. Yours open only one door at a time.

BERO. WHY AS!

OLD MAN. And rusty? Bent? Worn? Poisonous? When you're through the lock is broken? The room empty?

BERO. What is As?

OLD MAN. But why? Do you want to set up shop against me? Or against . . . others? (*He rolls his eyes towards the* MENDI-CANTS.) I think we have a conspiracy.

BERO. What is As?

OLD MAN. As Was, Is, Now, As Ever Shall be . . .

BERO (*quiet menace*). Don't play with me, Old Man.

OLD MAN. As doesn't change.

BERO (*increases pressure*). From what? To what?

OLD MAN (*choking, tugs at the swagger-stick.* BERO *lets go. The* OLD MAN *gets up, chafing his neck*). Do you know what one of those men once said? Let's send our gangrenous dressings by post to those sweet-smelling As agencies and homes. He sat down to compile a mailing list.

BERO. Yes?

OLD MAN. I understood.

BERO. What did you understand?

OLD MAN. As.

BERO (*violent reaction. Controls himself*). You are certified insane. Your fate creates no anxiety in anyone. Take a look at your companions – your humanity.

OLD MAN. I recognized it. A part of me identifies with every human being.

BERO. You'll be disillusioned soon enough.

OLD MAN. I do not harbour illusions. You do.

BERO (*genuinely astonished*). I? You say that of me. I, of all people?

OLD MAN. Oh, you are in good company. Even the cripple who is down-to-earth harbours illusions. Now, that's strange. I would have thought you would find that funny.

BERO. I do not need illusions. I control lives.

OLD MAN. Control – lives? What does that mean? Tell me what is the experience of it. Is it a taste? A smell? A feel? Do you have a testament that vindicates?

BERO. We have nothing that a petty mind can grasp. (*Pause.*) Try if you can, Old Man, to avoid twitching. Control belongs only to a few with the aptitude.

OLD MAN. One should always expect something new from the specialist. (*Contemptuously.*) Control!

BERO. Your old games won't help you. Forget that line.

OLD MAN. Throw me a new line then. Feed the drowning man a line.

BERO. You can swim.

OLD MAN (*turning to the others*). See? He's getting good. Swim? How?

BERO (*viciously*). We'll flood the place for you.

OLD MAN (*pleased*). You're getting very good, very good. It catches, you see. How do I swim? We'll flood the place. Or . . . is it merely in character? Is that it? Your peculiar little specialization. Perhaps that's it. So. When do you start?

BERO. Perhaps not at all. It would take too long.

OLD MAN (*nodding*). Y-e-s. And the place is not waterproof. I noticed rats. That means holes. You should see the rats.

BERO. They'll desert.

OLD MAN (*gazing round at the* MENDICANTS). I suppose so.

BERO. Or smoke you out. You will suffocate, slowly.

OLD MAN. Smoke. Smoke-screen. That's what it all is.

BERO. What?

OLD MAN. The pious pronouncements. Manifestos. Charades. At the bottom of it all humanity choking in silence.

BERO. You think a lot of yourself, don't you?

OLD MAN. Who else shall I think much of? You?

BERO. I control . . .

OLD MAN (*waves it aside*). Tell me something new. Or if you won't, these ones will. Aafaa!

AAFAA. What now?

OLD MAN. We are done with the flood. It never came. These midgets try to re-create the Flood but they lack the power. At least God had a reason. A damnable reason but at least he had a reason. And a good pump to clean up the mess. Not like these. What do you offer in place of the Flood?

AAFAA (*challenging*). Running water.

OLD MAN (*disgusted tone*). Nothing better?

AAFAA. You're dodging.

OLD MAN. Running water! (*He turns to the* CRIPPLE.) You deal with that. It's beneath my intellect.

CRIPPLE. Muddy. How do I get across it?

OLD MAN. God, they're all so self-centred. He means running progress. Faucets, pipes.

CRIPPLE. Can't reach the tap. Too high.

AAFAA. And who cares about you? Just who the hell do you think you are?

CRIPPLE (*stubbornly*). Too high.

OLD MAN (*smiles*). Like the price. See? Blindman?

BLINDMAN. Running water? Running mouths. Election promises.

OLD MAN (*to* BERO). See? Let's have a new one.

AAFAA. Electricity. (*Seeing* BLINDMAN *about to speak.*) And don't you tell me it's no good to you.

BLINDMAN. And whose fault is that? I wasn't born blind, you know.

CRIPPLE. Ho ho, remember that story of the blind man with a lamp?

GOYI. Don't tell me you went to school too?

AAFAA. What! Same old primer? Reader II or . . . was it Reader III?

CRIPPLE (*complacently*). Reader III, Elementary. Lamb and Wool Reader for Schools – well, something like that.

AAFAA. I bet you stopped at III.

CRIPPLE. No. Went up to four. Then I got the call of the road.

GOYI. I'll tell the story. A blind man went walking one day, carrying a lamp. Thereupon he met a neighbour. The neighbour stared, amazed . . .

AAFAA. A born fool.

CRIPPLE. I bet you would have found it queer too.

AAFAA. You forget I am a student of human peculiarities. Human peculiarities.

GOYI. Shut up, let me continue.

AAFAA. The neighbour said, Good blind neighbour, what good on earth is a lamp to you?

GOYI. Whereupon the blind man replied . . .

ALL TOGETHER (*in kindergarten voice*). I carry this lamp, good fellow, not that I may see but . . . (*Pause.*)

AAFAA. So that the whole world can see you when you try to

rob me. (*He bursts into his maniacal laughter, joined by the others.*)

OLD MAN (*reflectively*). A lamp has its uses.

AAFAA. So, electricity.

GOYI. Bleeah! Election promises.

CRIPPLE. What we want is individual manifestos.

AAFAA. Manifesto for every freak? General Electric!

OLD MAN. Electrocutes. Electric chair. Electrodes on the nerve-centres – your favourite pastime, I believe? Tell me something new. What hasn't been abused?

BERO (*has taken out his gun, weighs it significantly*). And lightning strikes. What about it?

OLD MAN. The boy learns. The boy learns.

BERO. Don't you dare patronize me. Answer me, what about it?

OLD MAN. That lightning strikes? It could strike you, no?

BERO. Yes.

OLD MAN (*quiet triumphant smile*). Then you're not omnipotent. You can't do a flood and you – (*Pause.*) – can't always dodge lightning. Why do you ape the non-existent one who can? Why do you ape nothing?

BERO. You tax my patience. Better watch out in future.

OLD MAN (*quietly*). The future?

BERO. The future, yes. The End . . .

OLD MAN. Justifies the meanness.

BERO (*again, angry reaction. He controls himself*). Just think of this – you have none.

OLD MAN (*calls after him*). Tell me something new. Tell me what is happening in the future. (*They all listen to* BERO's *footsteps receding.*) If he'd waited, I would have told him what's happening in the future. A faithful woman picking herbs for a smoke-screen on abuse.

Lights up sharply in the OLD WOMEN's *hut. No break in action.*

IYA AGBA (*screaming*). Abuse! Abuse! What do we do? Close
  our eyes and see nothing?

IYA MATE. Patience now. Patience.

IYA AGBA. What is it then! I see abominations. What do you
  see?

IYA MATE. The same, but . . .

IYA AGBA. Then what are we waiting for? Get ready the pot of
  fire.

IYA MATE. Do you think a little more time . . .?

IYA AGBA. To do worse? To do more? It's a good night for
  settling accounts.

IYA MATE. She's a good woman.

IYA AGBA. Get it ready. Get it ready. I'll not be a tool in their
  hands, not in this ripe state – No! Too much has fallen in
  their hands already, it's time to take it back. They spat on
  my hands when I held them out bearing gifts. Have you
  ever known it different?

IYA MATE. We hoped this might be.

IYA AGBA. Hope is dead, I must defend what is mine. Or let it
  die also. Let it be destroyed.

IYA MATE. Everything?

IYA AGBA. Everything. Everything they took from me.

IYA MATE. I think only of her.

IYA AGBA. She's a good woman and her heart is strong. And
  it is that kind who tire suddenly in their sleep and pass on to
  join their ancestors. What happens then?

IYA MATE. We can wait till then.

IYA AGBA. And I? Have you spoken to the ones below and did
  they tell you I shall still be among the living when her bones
  are rested.

IYA MATE. You leave me nothing to say.

IYA AGBA. There is nothing more to say. We pay our dues to
  earth in time, I also take back what is mine.

The clinic as last seen. Instant transition as before.

CRIPPLE (*singing*).
  I want my dues
  Not promises
  I want my dues
  Not promises . . .

AAFAA (*singing*). I want my dues. (*Stops.*) How about it, Old
  Man? I want my world tour. Old Man, you promised. I
  want that world tour you promised.

CRIPPLE. Promises. What else have we ever got from him?

GOYI. He got us the cigarettes anyway.

AAFAA. Raises a man's hopes for nothing. So where is this world
  tour you kept promising?

CRIPPLE. A Travelling Exhibition of As Grotesques, I remember.

AAFAA. You should, you illiterate reptile. You flung your
  crutches at his head because you thought it was an insult
  didn't you? Said he was making fun of you.

CRIPPLE. Why bring it up? The Blindman explained it. He
  said Grotesque only meant Greatest and I said I was sorry.

GOYI. He did too, I remember. And the Old Man also promised
  me top billing. (*Pause.*) I didn't want to ask at the time, but
  what is top billing, Blindman?

AAFAA. It means the Old Man would see that you got to the
  top of the ladder.

  Pause.

CRIPPLE. How do *I* get there, Aafaa?

AAFAA. Why ask me foolish questions you persistent little
  egotist? When the specialist told you you'd soon be doing
  better than you were when you had both legs, did you come
  to Aafaa for explanations?

GOYI. So? Are we getting the world tour or not?

CRIPPLE. Nitwit! As if he could even do anything about that
  now. Better forget it.

AAFAA. Old Man, you shouldn't have promised the travelling

show. (*Changing voice.*) Beat all known circuses hollow. I'll
take the wrappings off you and leave the world gasping.
What else . . .?

CRIPPLE. You've been pushed in the background too often.

GOYI. Always hidden away.

CRIPPLE (*coyly*). Not that we're shy.

GOYI. Always hidden away.

CRIPPLE. We're more decent than most. Hn-hn, than most.

AAFAA. Hidden under pension schemes you are.

GOYI. Tail-of-the-parade outings.

AAFAA. Behind the big drum.

CRIPPLE. Under royalty visits.

AAFAA (*graciously proffering his hand*). You may.

> GOYI *kisses his hand.*

CRIPPLE. Imperial commendations.

> AAFAA *unfurls the scrolls, slaps his tongue up and down.*

CRIPPLE. Unveiling of the plaque . . .

GOYI. Commemoration occasion . . .

AAFAA. Certificates of merit . . .

GOYI. Long-service medals . . .

> *The* CRIPPLE *dashes forward to the feet of* AAFAA *who takes
> medals from an invisible aide. His eyes roll from side to side,
> seeing no one.* GOYI *goes to him, taps him and points to the*
> CRIPPLE. AAFAA *tries but cannot make it. Finally he kisses*
> GOYI *on both cheeks, who then kisses the* CRIPPLE *on both
> cheeks. He pins the medal on* GOYI's *left shoulder, who then
> pins medal on the* CRIPPLE's *chest. All three cry: 'Speech'
> 'Speech' 'We want Him' 'We want Him' 'We want Him'
> rising to a crescendo. Finally* BLINDMAN *gets up, walks
> slowly downstage.*

BLINDMAN (*the speech should be varied with the topicality and
locale of the time*). It was our duty and a historical necessity. It

is our duty and a historical beauty. It shall always be. What we have, we hold. What though the wind of change is blowing over this entire continent, our principles and traditions – yes, must be maintained. For we are threatened, yes, we are indeed threatened. Excuse me, please, but we are entitled to match you history for history to the nearest half-million souls. Look at the hordes, I implore you. They stink. They eat garlic. What on earth have we in common with *them*? Understand me, please, understand me and do not misinterpret my intentions. The copper is quite incidental. Manganese? I don't know what it means. I always thought it was female for Kantagese. As for oil, I can't tell which is the margarine. If we don't stop them now, who knows but it may be our turn next moment. I ask you, do you want to wake up murdered in your beds? (*The others laugh.*) I assure you it's quite possible. No, please, it's no laughing matter. I mean . . . oh, I beg your pardon. You know what I mean, of course, do you want to wake up and find you've been . . . no I suppose that is also unlikely; better simply say . . . oh, well, look, strictly between you and me, all it boils down to is – would you want your daughter married to one of them? . . . It may happen, believe me, it may happen – if we're lucky. Rape is more natural to them than marriage. Even Confucius said it – if it must be, lie back and enjoy it. That coming from their greatest – er – er – atomic scientist is not a statement to be taken lightly. The black menace is no figment of my father's imagination. Look here . . . have you had the experience of watching them – breed? No no, I mean . . . I don't mean being actually *there* . . . please please please, I was referring to statistics, statistics. We feed those statistics into a computer and here is what they say . . . What we have, we hold. What though the wind of change is blowing over this entire continent, our principles and traditions – yes, must be maintained. For we are threatened. Yes, we are indeed threatened. Excuse me, but we are entitled to match you

history for history to the nearest half-million souls. Look at
the hordes, I implore you. They stink. They eat garlic . . .

As BLINDMAN *begins the re-run, the other* MENDICANTS
commence their chant, AAFAA *taking the lead. The song goes
faster and faster and louder and they clap him down until*
BLINDMAN *gives up and bows.*

As Is Was Now
As Ever Shall Be

Bi o ti wa   etc. etc.
Ni yi o se wa
Bi o ti wa
Ni yi o se wa

They give BLINDMAN *a round of applause while he feels
his way towards the* OLD MAN.

BLINDMAN. I hope I didn't do too badly.

OLD MAN (*sighs, turns to face him*). No. It was quite a good
effort.

BLINDMAN. It was rather like old times.

OLD MAN. Very much like old times.

CRIPPLE. Hey, listen. The Old Man was pleased.

AAFAA. I should bloody well hope so. It was just like old
times.

CRIPPLE. My feelings exactly. Just like old times.

GOYI. It . . . was . . . just . . . like old times.

AAFAA. Yes. So why risk putting us here together?

OLD MAN. Because . . . we are together in As. (*He rises slowly.*)
As Is, and the System is its mainstay though it wear a
hundred masks and a thousand outward forms. And because
you are within the System, the cyst in the System that irri-
tates, the foul gurgle of the cistern, the expiring function of
a faulty cistern and are part of the material for re-formulat-
ing the mind of a man into the necessity of the moment's

political As, the moment's scientific As, metaphysic As, sociologic As, economic, recreative ethical As, you-cannot-es-cape! There is but one constant in the life of the System and that constant is AS. And what can you pit against the priesthood of that constant deity, its gospellers, its enforcement agency. And even if you say unto them, do I not know you, did I not know you in rompers, with leaky nose and smutty face? Did I not know you thereafter, know you in the haunt of cat-houses, did I not know you rifling the poorboxes in the local church, did I not know you dissolving the night in fumes of human self-indulgence simply simply simply did I not know you, do you not defecate, fornicate, prevaricate when heaven and earth implore you to abdicate and are you not prey to headaches, indigestion, colds, disc displacement, ingrowing toe-nail, dysentery, malaria, flatfoot, corns and chilblains. Simply simply, do I not know you Man like me? Then shall they say unto you, I am chosen, restored, re-designated and re-destined and further further shall they say unto you, you heresiarchs of the System arguing questioning querying weighing puzzling insisting rejecting upon you all shall we practise, without passion –

MENDICANTS. Practise . . .

OLD MAN. With no ill-will . . .

MENDICANTS. Practise . . .

OLD MAN. With good conscience . . .

MENDICANTS. Practise . . .

OLD MAN. That the end shall . . .

MENDICANTS. Practise . . .

OLD MAN. Justify the meanness . . .

MENDICANTS. Practise . . .

OLD MAN. Without emotion . . .

MENDICANTS. Practise . . .

OLD MAN. Without human ties . . .

MENDICANTS. Practise . . .

OLD MAN. Without – no – Lest there be self-doubting . . .

MENDICANTS. Practise . . . As Was the Beginning, As Is, Now, As Ever Shall Be, World Without.

As the OLD MAN *slowly resumes his seat,* AAFAA *rises, speaking.*

AAFAA. In the beginning was the Priesthood, and the Priesthood was one. Then came schism after schism by a parcel of schismatic ticks in the One Body of Priesthood, the political priesthood went right the spiritual priesthood went left or vice versa the political priesthood went back the spiritual priesthood went fore and vice versa the political priesthood went down the spiritual priesthood went up or vice versa the loyalty of homo sapiens was never divided for two parts of a division make a whole and there was no hole in the monolithic solidarity of two halves of the priesthood. No, there was no division. The loyalty of homo sapiens regressed into himself, himself his little tick-tock self, self-ticking, self-tickling, self-tackling problems that belonged to the priesthood spiritual and political while they remained the sole and indivisible one. Oh, look at him, Monsieur l'homme sapiens, look at the lone usurper of the ancient rights and privileges of the priesthood, (*The* CRIPPLE *makes an obscene gesture.* AAFAA *registers shock.*) look at the dog in dogma raising his hindquarters to cast the scent of his individuality on the lamp-post of Destiny! On him practise Practise! Practise! As was the Beginning –

MENDICANTS. Practise . . .

AAFAA. As Is . . .

MENDICANTS. Practise . . .

AAFAA. Now . . .

MENDICANTS. Practise . . .

AAFAA. As Ever Shall Be . . .

MENDICANTS. Practise. . .

AAFAA. World without . . .

MENDICANTS. Practise! Practise! Practise!

From the chorus of 'Practise' they slip into their chant, softly.

OLD MAN (*rising again*). On the cyst in the system, you cysts, you damnable warts . . . (*He freezes with his arm raised towards the next scene as if in benediction.*)

The 'Bi o ti wa' chant continues underneath and AAFAA *continues with his spastic dance somewhat muted all through the next scene.*

IYA AGBA *and* IYA MATE *have arrived in front of* SI BERO's *house, the latter carrying the pot of glowing coals. She places it on the ground.*

IYA AGBA. Call her name.
IYA MATE. Si Bero!

SI BERO *comes out a few moments later, obviously roused from sleep. She notices first the pot of coals, then makes out figures of the two women in the dark. She shrinks back.*

Don't be afraid, daughter. No harm will come to you.

IYA AGBA. We thought it was time for a visit. Bid us welcome so we can go about our business.

SI BERO. It's . . . it's an unusual time for earth-mothers to visit their daughters.

IYA AGBA. Not if they have debts to collect. Say how you want it done, woman.

SI BERO. Debts! No, not him. Don't touch him, my mothers.

IYA AGBA. I waste no strength on carrion. I leave him to earth's rejection.

SI BERO. Give me more time. I have the power of a mother with him.

IYA MATE (*gently*). We waited as long as we could, daughter.

IYA AGBA. Time has run out. Do you think time favours us? Can I sleep easy when my head is gathering mould on your shelves?

SI BERO. You said yourself nothing goes to waste.

IYA AGBA. What is used for evil is also put to use. Have I not sat with the knowledge of abuse these many days and kept the eyes of my mind open?

IYA MATE. It cannot wait, daughter. Evil hands soon find a use for the best of things.

SI BERO. Let it wait my mothers, let it wait.

IYA AGBA (*angrily*). Rain falls and seasons turn. Night comes and goes – do you think they wait for the likes of you? I warned you when we took you in the fold . . .

SI BERO. I'll repay it all I promise . . .

IYA AGBA. I said this gift is not one you gather in one hand. If your other hand is fouled the first withers also.

IYA MATE. That is how we met it. No one can change that.

SI BERO (*clutching* IYA MATE *around the knees*). Not you too. You were never as hard as she.

IYA MATE. Nothing we can do, daughter, nothing but follow the way as we met it.

SI BERO. And the good that is here? Does that count for nothing?

IYA AGBA. We'll put that into the test. Let us see how it takes to fire.

SI BERO. Fire?

IYA AGBA. It is only the dying embers of an old woman's life. The dying embers of earth as we knew it. Is that anything to fear?

SI BERO. We laboured hard together.

IYA AGBA. So does the earth on which I stand. And on which your house stands, woman. If you want the droppings of rodents on your mat I can only look on. But my head still fills your room from wall to wall and dirty hands touch it . . .

SI BERO. No, no, nobody but myself . . .

IYA AGBA. I need to sleep in peace . . .

She raises the pot suddenly to throw the embers into the store. BERO *steps out at that moment, gun in hand, bearing down on* IYA AGBA.

OLD MAN (*his voice has risen to a frenzy*). Practise, Practise, Practise . . . on the cyst in the system . . .

BERO *is checked in stride by the voice. He now hesitates between the two distractions.*

. . . you cyst, you cyst, you splint in the arrow of arrogance, the dog in doma, tick of a heretic, the tick in politics, the mock of democracy, the mar of marxism, a tic of the fanatic, the boo in buddhism, the ham in Mohammed, the dash in the criss-cross of Christ, a dot on the i of ego an ass in the mass, the ash in ashram, a boot in kibbutz, the pee of priesthood, the peepee of perfect priesthood, oh how dare you raise your hindquarters you dog of dogma and cast the scent of your existence on the lamp-post of Destiny you HOLE IN THE ZERO of NOTHING!

CRIPPLE. I have a question.

OLD MAN (*turns slowly towards the interruption*). It's the dreamer.

CRIPPLE. I have a question.

OLD MAN. Black that Zero! (AAFAA, GOYI *and* BLINDMAN *begin to converge on the* CRIPPLE.)

CRIPPLE. I have a question.

OLD MAN. Shut that gaping hole or we fall through it.

CRIPPLE. I have a question.

The MENDICANTS' *chorus 'Practise' as they beat him.*

OLD MAN. Stop him cold, stop him dead! Let me hear the expiring suction of an imperfect system.

CRIPPLE. My question is . . .

AAFAA *snatches one of* GOYI's *crutches. In the background the sound of* BERO *breaking down the door.* AAFAA *brings down crutch on the* CRIPPLE's *head.*

OLD MAN. Stop him! Fire! Fire! Riot! Hot line! Armageddon!

As he shouts, the OLD MAN *snatches the* SURGEON'S *coat from where it is hanging, puts it on, dons cap, pulls on the gloves and picks up a scalpel.*

OLD MAN (*at the top of his voice*). Bring him over here. (*He dons mask.*) Bring him over here. Lay him out. Stretch him flat. Strip him bare. Bare! Bare! Bare his soul! Light the stove!

They heave him onto the table and hold him down while the OLD MAN *rips the shirt open to bare the* CRIPPLE'S *chest.* BERO *rushes in and takes in the scene, raises his pistol and aims at the* OLD MAN.

OLD MAN. Let us taste just what makes a heretic tick.

He raises the scalpel in a motion for incision. BERO *fires. The* OLD MAN *spins, falls face upwards on the table as the* CRIPPLE *slides to the ground from under him. A momentary freeze on stage. Then* SI BERO *rushes from the* OLD WOMEN *towards the surgery. Instantly* IYA AGBA *hurls the embers into the store and thick smoke belches out from the doorway gradually filling out the stage. Both women walk calmly away as* SI BERO *reappears in the doorway of the surgery. The* MENDICANTS *turn to look at her, break gleefully into their favourite song. The* OLD WOMEN *walk past their hut, stop at the spot where the* MENDICANTS *were first seen and look back towards the surgery. The song stops in mid-word and the lights snap out simultaneously.*

Bi o ti wa
Ni yio se wa

                Bi o ti wa

Ni yio se wa
Bi o ti wa l'atete ko.

THE END

Methuen World Classics

Aeschylus (two volumes)
Jean Anouilh
John Arden
Arden & D'Arcy
Aristophanes (two volumes)
Peter Barnes
Brendan Behan
Aphra Behn
Edward Bond (four volumes)
Bertolt Brecht (three volumes)
Howard Brenton (two volumes)
Büchner
Bulgakov
Calderón
Anton Chekhov
Caryl Churchill (two volumes)
Noël Coward (five volumes)
Sarah Daniels
Eduardo De Filippo
David Edgar (three volumes)
Euripides (three volumes)
Dario Fo
Michael Frayn (two volumes)
Max Frisch
Gorky
Harley Granville Barker
Henrik Ibsen (six volumes)
Lorca (three volumes)
Marivaux
Mustapha Matura
David Mercer
Arthur Miller (three volumes)
Anthony Minghella
Molière
Tom Murphy (two volumes)
Peter Nichols (two volumes)
Clifford Odets
Joe Orton
Louise Page
A. W. Pinero
Luigi Pirandello
Stephen Poliakoff
Terence Rattigan (two volumes)
Ntozake Shange
Sophocles (two volumes)
Wole Soyinka
David Storey
August Strindberg (three volumes)
J. M. Synge
Ramón del Valle-Inclán
Frank Wedekind
Oscar Wilde